N̸E

UNIFORM
DECISIONS

UNIFORM DECISIONS

MY LIFE IN THE LAPD

and the NORTH HOLLYWOOD SHOOTOUT

JOHN CAPRARELLI
WITH LEE MINDHAM

Uniform Decisions
By John Caprarelli
With Lee Mindham

ISBN: 978-0-9849167-0-2

Published by End of Watch Publishing
Los Angeles, CA
www.endofwatch.com

The contents of this book are based on actual experiences as recalled and/or investigated to the best ability of the authors. Some of the names of those involved have been changed. Comments of a personal nature regarding any persons or organizations are the sole opinions of the authors. No legal advice is intended.

Editor: Tracy Irons-Georges
Cover design: Lynn Caprarelli
Bank of America cover photograph: Gene Blevins

Printed in the United States of America

To my wife, Lynn, and two sons,
John and Jim:
Evidence beyond a shadow of a doubt
How blessed I am.

CONTENTS

INTRODUCTION

It's not easy to write about one's career and turn those memories into words that accurately describe them.

That's not for a lack of eligible "excitement," if you choose to call it that. My career had more than its fair share, but translating emotions into words is not always an easy task.

Putting my story down on paper was never something I chomped at the bit to do, but after many years of urging by family, friends and acquaintances, I decided the time was right.

Is it worth the price of this book? I think so.

My career was anything but ordinary. During twenty-seven years with the Los Angeles Police Department, I experienced many an extraordinary day at work, including involvement in a modern-day "Shootout at the OK Corral."

It's said that working the streets as a police officer is hours of boredom sprinkled with seconds of terror. I can vouch for that. It was quite a ride.

John Caprarelli

ACKNOWLEDGMENTS

Writing this book has been a personal journey and a team effort, with my family being my greatest support. Special thanks go to my wife, Lynn, for gently pushing me onward to tell a story that I would not have otherwise. Her tireless work and patience in putting my words into print and designing the book's cover and layout highlight her continued unwavering love and support.

I thank my co-author, Lee Mindham. His research and attention to detail were invaluable, his enthusiasm and wit a continuing light at the end of the tunnel.

I also thank our editor, Tracy Irons-Georges; our proofreaders Judi Irons, Kym Irons, Madeline Irons and Rusty Irons; Adrian Martinez, for his research and technical support; and Gene Blevins, for the use of his photographs.

PROLOGUE

With my knees pressed against the back of the driver's seat, I can feel its metal frame. The atmosphere inside the car is electric, crackling with the ozone of anticipation and masked fear. The police radio strapped under the dash is spewing out a torrent of messages, updates and yells overrunning one another in a mass of urgency and desperation. It's a morning of utter chaos in North Hollywood.

I turn my head to the officer in the seat next to me. Facing forward, eyes wide open and stone faced, he slowly looks to the floor as if bowing his head and momentarily closes his eyes as if saying a quick prayer. Not a bad idea after just being shot at and about to face what is yet to come.

As he raises his head a bead of sweat, as if in slow motion, rolls down his nose, catching the sunlight as it falls to oblivion between his feet.

The neck of my own shirt is soaked as well, and I can feel the beads on my face making their own journeys downward. It reminds me of my summers as a youth working up a sweat pushing the lawn mower under the hot sun. It isn't the scent of freshly cut grass permeating the air today, however. Another scent intrudes, a dark and pungent odor that has no place among that soft reminiscence: burnt gunpowder.

Jolted back to reality, here we are crawling northbound along Agnes Avenue, four of us in an unmarked police car. Suddenly, gunshots erupt and a white Chevrolet Celebrity comes bounding through the intersection just ahead. The human silence in the car is broken.

"THERE! THERE!" yells the front seat passenger, pointing at the fleeing car.

My head snaps up, eyes catching the tail end of the Chevy, trunk open and flapping as it picks up speed. Our driver stomps on the gas pedal, and the cruiser leaps forward like an eager cheetah after its prey.

As we approach the intersection, I glance to my left—an automatic, mentally programmed check for traffic. It isn't traffic that I get a glimpse of, rather that of a tractor-trailer parked at the curb with somebody moving underneath, someone who obviously doesn't belong there.

PROLOGUE

Without any thought process, my instincts take over. I yell, "Hold it!" Waiting for what seems like an eternity, I fling the car door open and jump out before the car comes to a complete stop.

Quickly but cautiously I cross the road, gun in hand and scanning the area in front of me for any other movement or sound. There is nothing else, just the movement under the truck and the sound of my own footsteps. Suddenly, another staccato bark of large-caliber automatic gunfire snarls out from close by, followed by muted "cracks" of smaller arms returning fire.

Someone has to stop this, and I quickly realize I have the chance to do just that.

As I near the corner, a white metal fence standing waist high and rounding to my left catches my eye. The thought of its thin, sparsely arranged pillars being any sort of "cover" exits my mind as fast as it enters. So, here I stand, alone and exposed on Archwood Street facing this brown tractor-trailer unit. Underneath: my target.

Dressed all in black, resplendent with ski mask, body armor and an AK-47 assault rifle, is a wounded and highly aggressive suspect in flight. Like a cut rattlesnake, he is angrily firing at anything that moves, pinning everybody down—my brothers in arms, my friends, even innocent civilians who have happened to get within his striking distance.

As he squats down, facing away from me and shuffling his position slightly, I raise my 9mm Beretta. I begin to feel as though I'm being submerged in honey. Time becomes sticky, slow and tangible.

The muzzle of my weapon gradually rises past my chest level. I can see the front sight come up higher, seeking a straight shot at this monster's back.

In a heartbeat, it all starts to go wrong.

He has seen me over his shoulder. I am now a threat, a threat to his life and very close. I have been caught creeping and the world, except for the two of us, will now cease to exist until this tableau has played out. Only one of us will walk away; only one will survive. A few seconds ago, I'd have bet it would be me going home that night, but now I'm not so sure.

My breathing slows despite a massive surge of adrenaline flowing through my veins. I try to move faster but can't, like those dreams when you try to run from some threat and your body just can't respond. I am too slow, and he's going to get the drop on me.

I can see it all, the muzzle of the AK-47, the 100-round drum, the ground littered with spent casings and the dark eyes fixated on me, full of loathing. He looks like an angry cobra puffed up and ready to strike.

My breathing slows even more; I feel like I'm not getting enough oxygen. Tunnel vision closes in.

Why can't I breathe?!

With my gun now pointed squarely at the center of his chest, I jerk back on the trigger; the metal pressing against my right forefinger.

PROLOGUE

This is it! I got you after all! Or so I think.

Nothing! The trigger will not move.

I squeeze harder. Again, nothing. It feels jammed solid.

WHAT IS HAPPENING?

The muzzle of his rifle is now squarely on me. Another second, maybe a half, and it will be all over.

I glance at my weapon in confused amazement. I feel like I haven't drawn a breath in minutes. My head is spinning, my chest constricted, and I can hear the blood roaring through my ears.

I give it one last chance and pull back on the trigger with all that I have.

Nothing. Not even a millimeter.

Realizing that it is probably over, I look up from where the rounds of my 9mm should have gone and then at his face. Looking at his eyes, I can see under his sweat-sodden ski mask that the corners of his eyes are crinkled. He is smiling at me! With his leather-gloved finger curled around the AK-47's trigger, it seems as though his jaw is mouthing something from behind the ski mask.

Panic courses through me and everything goes black as the world seems instantly yanked from me.

Am I shot? Is this it? What happened?

Drawing one long rasp of fresh air, I feel like I have just popped to the surface after too deep of a dive in some murky waters. It is dark, I am covered in sweat, and my heart is pounding like a jackhammer.

Where am I?

My vision clears. The panic steps down half-a-notch as I see moonlight through our bedroom window, a soft night breeze stirring the half-open curtains.

My wife's hand touches my shoulder as she asks, "You okay?"

I can hear in her voice that she is wide awake and knows I had the nightmare again.

"Yeah, just another dream," I reply. "I'm fine."

We both know that is not true. There is an increasing menace, one we would not understand much about or know how to handle until it had already run its course.

I climb out of bed. I feel like a long distance runner at the end of a race, physically and mentally spent. The nightmare was like an adrenaline rush with an abrupt "hit the ground with no parachute" end.

Quietly, I make my way downstairs without turning on the lights and get a long drink of cold water. Standing in the darkness, I know there is no more sleep in store for me tonight.

I move to the living room, slump into my favorite end of the sofa and, with haunting memories to ponder, realize it is from here that I will watch the dawn break once again.

PROLOGUE

My name is John Caprarelli. I was a police officer with the Los Angeles Police Department.

This is my story.

CHAPTER ONE

OUT OF THE ORDINARY

There's a term I favor, a sequence of words that rolls nicely off the tongue, a phrase that I believe adequately sums up what a cop's career, especially in Los Angeles, is all about: riding the bullet.

Like a bullet fired from a gun, a cop's career can fly straight, true and unimpeded, to gently fall far from view, its energy and time spent and undamaged.

Those cops are the lucky ones, the vast majority who go through the gauntlet receiving maybe a scrape or two, never firing their weapons in defense of life or suffering any major injuries or traumas. They remain relatively unaffected by the situations they face as "a badge." Yeah, they are the lucky ones.

The flip side to that particular coin is that a cop's career can be totally different, his or her own particular bullet being a ricochet slamming wildly into one intense event, bouncing hard and tumbling unpredictably to the next.

There is no way to tell which particular bullet one will "ride" when signing up for the job. It's all how you roll the dice and how you're wired. Some can handle a wild ride; some cannot and sometimes see a rather short career.

Me? Well I came through, I survived. Twenty-seven years saw me ride a pretty wild bullet of my own. Admittedly I was bounced and bucked pretty hard, but I clung on and I'm here now to give you a glimpse inside what it was like to be a first responder, a cop in one of America's largest and most diverse cities.

Being a cop is not for everybody. It takes a person with a certain mentality, the same way it is for a person who joins the military, fire department or ranks of emergency medical professionals. The police department wasn't something I grew up longing to join but, unknown to me, that certain mentality was in my blood, taking me on a rather circuitous route to end where I did.

Before getting into that though, I want to take you back to the early days of my life.

When I was a child, my name would have been found in the "Average Everyday American Kid" column.

My father was of Italian descent. Raised in Providence, Rhode Island, and moving west to Los Angeles in the mid-1950's, he worked in the banking industry. My mother came from an Irish and English background in Fort Fairfield, Maine, and moved to Los Angeles around the same time to continue a nursing career. One day she walked into the bank where my father worked as a teller, and the rest is history.

I was born in 1957, and after a couple years of apartment jumping, my parents bought a house in the San Fernando Valley. It was a relatively crime-free area at the time, and my life, as any child's should be, was idyllic. Through my childhood, I was sufficient in physical abilities and academics, but not blessed enough to have either in remarkable portions.

It turns out that God was saving some generous blessings for me later in life.

For the time being, I enjoyed childhood, playing with friends on the block, and when they weren't around I could be found with my plastic green soldiers and tanks re-enacting battles from old war movies for hours on end. John Wayne, a stand-up guy and always on the winning side, was usually my favorite hero leading the charge. It was the good guys and the bad guys fighting it out, which I think planted a seed in my mind.

The time came when, like many boys in their younger years, I wanted to be a fireman.

The large, shiny red trucks that commanded right of way with their flashing lights and blaring sirens never failed to captivate my attention. I wondered what it must be like to be riding on one of those. Over time, it wasn't just the trucks that caught my attention. I also thought of the camaraderie that must exist in such a profession—a bunch of guys all working together for the same cause helping people, saving people. I was sold. That's what I wanted to do. It was a dream that I would hold onto for quite a long time.

With education being very important to my parents, my early years were spent in private schools in the San Fernando Valley. While I was in junior high school, we moved to a newer development in nearby Tujunga, a picturesque community nestled in the foothills of the San Gabriel Mountains. Hastily enrolling me in the local public school for ninth grade, my parents quickly realized that I needed a more challenging environment for learning. They presented me with two choices for high school: Flintridge Preparatory School, a prestigious all-boys school in La Cañada, and Village Christian School, a smaller co-ed school in Sun Valley whose curriculum revolved around the teachings of the Bible. I was interested in two things at that time: sports and girls. Flintridge had the better sports program, but Village Christian was still the easy choice.

Playing sports in high school, I found out that, despite bouts with asthma, I was a pretty good athlete. The adrenaline rush of competing and winning was addicting. I excelled in basketball and football and even got the attention of a few scouts, but I was just a bit too short and too thin to earn a sports scholarship. My sports career ended at graduation.

My teenage years overlapped the end of the so-called hippie era. The Vietnam War was raging in Asia while the "free love" movement raged against it back at home. I was intrigued with the whole hippie thing. The music was a big draw. Black lights with fluorescent posters were something new, and the whole idea of peace and harmony seemed like a good one.

I grew my hair as long as my parents would allow—which wasn't much. I didn't fight them though, because I knew that in the end the school dress code couldn't be trumped anyway.

My parents were very supportive of me, taking an active interest in my extracurricular activities. When I showed a passion and aptitude for photography, my father even built a darkroom in our garage and taught me to develop and print my own photographs.

Was I going to be the next Alfred Eisenstaedt? Or maybe a war photographer traipsing through a foreign land with a camera slung around my neck and a joint dangling from the corner of my mouth? No way. As much as the hippie movement captivated me, the drugs side of it never held an interest. I never understood how anyone could put such dangerous substances into their body. I had my mother the nurse to thank for that. I can still remember her saying "It just takes once," referring to the possibility of losing your life by toying with a drug even once. It really stuck with me.

I didn't go through a rebellious time like many of my friends. In fact, I had come to believe and accept the Christian teachings I was learning at Village Christian. However, out of wrong expectations and ignorance, I didn't let those teachings fully take hold. I put the whole faith thing on the back burner, but a recurring reminder, a subconscious "tapping on the shoulder," would follow me for many years.

The best thing about high school was meeting my future wife, Lynn, in the tenth grade. One day between classes, trying to act cool with my buddies, I saw her standing nearby talking to some friends. Her carefree shag hairstyle and crystal blue eyes snagged me like a fish hook. I caught her taking an extra glance in my direction, and, with a little persistence, we were eventually "going steady." Years later, I learned that her extra glance was not one of romantic interest but to see who was doing such a fine job of embarrassing himself. It didn't matter. The end justified the means.

Despite Lynn's transfer to another school in our junior year, we remained a couple, and about a year after graduating high school, on November 6, 1976, we married. I was nineteen, and she was eighteen. A lot of people said it wouldn't last, whispers we heard standing in the reception line at our wedding. I didn't care though. I was so happy, and you couldn't have dragged the smile off my face with a team of wild horses. We were joyfully looking toward our future together, not only as husband and wife but also as best friends.

With me employed as an assistant night manager at a Bob's Big Boy Restaurant and Lynn as a bank teller at Home Savings, we took up residence in a one-bedroom apartment in the San Fernando Valley.

It was only a couple of miles from the fire station where Lynn's uncle, Chris Irons, served as a captain with the Los

Angeles City Fire Department. Crossing paths with him around town and at family functions reminded me of my childhood dreams and rekindled my thoughts of becoming a firefighter. But with Lynn working days at the bank and me putting in excessive hours at the restaurant at night, those thoughts would be buried for another five years. We scraped by financially. I later worked as a pharmaceuticals delivery driver and then a motion picture film lab technician. They were decent jobs, but that was about it.

When my first son was born in 1980, I began to realize that I needed a more solid, stable and profitable foundation on which my family and I could ground ourselves. That was the impetus for me to finally act on my thoughts about joining the fire department. I hooked up with Lynn's Uncle Chris, who took me under his wing and began preparing me for the testing process, both mentally and physically.

At the time, retirements from the fire department were at low ebb. This, coupled with the department's other hiring policies then, made things slow going.

Time continued to fly by, and with talk of us having another child, I eventually added a night-time security guard job at the ABC Entertainment Center in Century City. Eight hours at the film lab during the day followed by eight hours as a guard walking a beat were exhausting, but we needed the money.

Forgetting for a moment some traffic citations I got in my early "hot rod" days, my first involvement with LAPD officers doing their job was during one long, cold night in Century City.

A silent burglar alarm, known in LAPD jargon as a "Code 30," had been activated in one of the buildings and the police automatically dispatched. Nervously pumped up at the thought of burglars nearby, I was a little perplexed at how nonchalant the officers were when they showed up, actually cracking a few jokes as they walked up to the offices. They took a quick look around to see if there were any kicked-in doors or smashed windows and then left me standing there, with raised eyebrows, as they joked their way back to their cruiser and drove away.

I remember thinking, "Well, that was quick!" No bullhorns, battering rams or SWAT team to storm in and apprehend the burglars who I was sure were inside cleaning the place out? No helicopters or searchlights? Nope, just a couple of wisecracking old-timers who had handled this same type of call a hundred times before.

I didn't know at the time that over ninety percent of "Code 30's" were false alarms, or that years later I would end up handling hundreds of them myself in the same way those two officers did, jokes and all.

It was just a few months later at a wedding reception that I met a gentleman new to my wife's side of the family who was a sergeant with the LAPD. When my ongoing and increasingly frustrating attempts at becoming a firefighter became the topic of conversation, he noted that there were numerous police department vacancies coming up and asked if I had ever thought of becoming a police officer instead. I hadn't, and not much more was discussed at that point, but the bug had been put in my ear.

I later recalled the two officers who had responded to the Code 30 in Century City, and my curiosity began to take off. As days went by, I started remembering all the *Adam-12* and *Dragnet* TV shows I watched in the past, as well as movies like *The New Centurions*.

Could I do that type of work?

That police sergeant apparently thought I could and so I started over, trading the pursuit of riding those shiny red trucks for patrolling within the confines of a black-and-white.

CHAPTER TWO

SELECTION

My shoes were nervously tapping quiet acapellas on the tile floor. They seemed to be on autopilot and wouldn't stop even if I wanted them to. Five months had gone by, and it was now D-Day.

Nothing could calm me down.

It was June, 1982, and I was inside a bland, square room deep in the white brick-and-glass-clad LAPD Parker Center in downtown Los Angeles. The white-noise hum of the air conditioner, soft murmur of conversations and impatient shuffling of chairs shared the air with the musty smell of an old classroom harboring aged dry books and chalk dust. Sitting among sixty others anxious for their own breaks to unfold, my mind raced: "C'mon already! Let's get this show on the road!"

I had spent those previous months working my way through the application process; a tedious, taxing time which took me to a whole new level in exercising patience. It wasn't the typical routine of fill out a form, do a quick interview and, if they like you, you're in. It was a rigorous, in-depth and structured set of tests, investigations and interviews. That wasn't surprising to me: I was trying to become a police officer, not a door-to-door salesman.

There was the written, the physical, the medical, the psychological, the background and the all-important oral interview. In between each test was a tedious wait, wondering if I'd passed and been recommended for the next phase or if I'd been disqualified. Time was the only thing to contend with in getting through the written and physical abilities tests. The psychological was rather interesting but also completed with no problems.

The medical produced a glitch, however. I remember sitting in front of the city doctor during my medical exam and hearing him say that my blood pressure was a little high. He would need to get additional medical history from my personal doctor. I thought to myself, "Isn't everybody's blood pressure reading a little high sitting in front of you and knowing that your 'OK' or 'Not OK' determines his future?" Eventually, he gave me the all-clear, but not until after several days of nervous fretting on my part.

Then there was the background investigation, which held its own nerve-wracking surprise. As I arrived home one evening between jobs, Lynn told me the background investigator had been by the house earlier that day and interviewed her. That got my blood pumping and my mind racing, wondering how it went. Wanting a complete breakdown, my whole focus went to Lynn. When I looked at her, however, I felt as though my chances of being hired were dashed for sure.

A day earlier, after leaning over to play with our one-year-old son John on the bed, I stood up just as Lynn was approaching from behind with diaper in hand to change him. I accidentally smacked her square in the eye with the back of my head, resulting in quite a shiner. Later that same evening, John accidentally fell and hit his eye on the edge of a table and joined his mother with a matching black eye. Lynn took the next day off from work and kept John home from the baby-sitter's, so coincidentally they were there to open the door for the investigator.

I paused as I realized how a good old-fashioned black eye could blossom to eyebrow-raising prominence. The background investigator surely must have thought I was some sort of abuser and definitely not qualified to be a "peace" officer. I felt sick, but after a few reassuring words from Lynn, the color came back to my face. The investigator had interrupted her as she attempted to explain the situation to him, telling her that he had already talked to enough people to know that I would never be the type of person to do such a thing intentionally. He noted rather humorously the timing between this incident and the interview but again assured her that it was a non-issue. I felt pulled from the precipice again.

After making it through all the checks and hoops to that point, "The Oral" was the next and last in line. You got only one shot, and you had to make it count. This interview decided how far up or down the hiring list you would be placed. If you ranked high enough, you got the invite. If you didn't, well you'd be going back to your old job—or, in my case, jobs.

Struck down by a case of nerves on that day? Oh well. Too bad! Go through the whole process and try again next year.

Saying I was nervous during my interview would be putting it rather mildly, but afterward I felt I had done well enough to get high up in the ranking. Waiting for the results to come in the mail was the most torturous time yet. When the letter finally arrived, it wasn't the news I'd been hoping for: I was placed on the alternate list, the backup list they would pick from if anyone didn't show up the day they handed out the jobs. I was crushed and thought to myself, "You've got to be kidding! Who wouldn't show up after going through that whole process and being offered the job?"

It felt like someone rubbing salt in the wound. Injured pride and disbelief stung at me. First, the fire department slipped through my fingers and now the same thing seemed to be happening with the police department. There was a lifeline, however. I was still an alternate and, desperately searching for hope, noted I was first on that list. I wasn't going to give up. I'd had enough of burning the candle at both ends. I needed this job—the money, the security, the future. I would be there.

I was surrounded by a sea of confident-looking faces, most of them reasonably secure in hearing their names being called. Then there were us alternates, each trying to maintain a façade of composure while battling the shadows of doubt inside. My only consolation was that my name was number one on The List. My nerves played with me as I sat there, thinking again about who on earth would go through all those months of tests, get the invitation to be here and not turn up on the all-important final day? Who would be that crazy? The thought kept charging around my head as the names started being called, the lucky ones, the chosen ones.

After a while, the monotony of "Here!" for replies was broken. A name was called without answer. It was called again; there was still no answer. My ears perked up.

This is it. A no-show! Here we go! Optimism coursed through me now. The next thing I should hear was my name. I glanced at the door, half expecting some sweating, panting and red-faced guy to come barging through while apologizing for being late. Nope, there was no one. My optimism climbed another notch, but instead of going to the alternate list, they resumed calling names from the original list. My heart sank. In desperation, I wanted to jump up and shout, 'HEY! What about the alternate list? You skipped a spot!" but I stayed glued to my seat, my heart pounding so hard I wondered if anyone could hear it.

They continued down the list, with every second giving more time for the no-show to burst into the room and dash my hopes. As I twisted in my seat and became more anxious, a low anger born of frustration began growing inside me. Now I was getting irked: "How long are they going to give this guy?" Finally, it was the end of the list— crunch time.

They called his name one last time, and again there was no reply.

That was it! Out came the alternate list.

"Caprarelli, John"

It caught me a little off guard. Did they really say my name? Then I heard it again: "Caprarelli, John."

Keeping my outward composure as well as I could, I replied with a solid "Here!" Inside I was yelling, "Yeah! I made it!" I had my foot in the door. I was going to the Los Angeles Police Academy.

I left Parker Center on cloud nine. Returning to work to sit and operate the film-processing machine for the rest of the day before heading home seemed like forever. I wanted to tell Lynn the good news.

When I got home that night, I could smell dinner cooking. Lynn met me at the door with two glasses, a bottle of champagne and a smile on her face. How did she know? Was it a woman's intuition? It would be a pretty risky guess to make. It appeared she had more faith in me than I knew.

The euphoria of making it through the selection process, and then being chosen, lasted several days. I would not have long to savor the moment, though. A new challenge awaited me, and things were going to be different. The academy started in just two weeks, and soon I would find out if I had what it took to make it through the training.

CHAPTER THREE

ACADEMY DAYS

The house where you live, the building where you work, your favorite restaurant—they all have their histories. Their walls contain the memories and secrets of those who have passed through that space before you.

The LAPD academy at Elysian Park is no different. Recruits who step through those fabled stone towers and into the facility itself cannot help but be reminded of the history that surrounds them.

I can recall many times pausing between classes and taking in the scenery—that infamous gate, the stone walls, the immaculate flower beds, the Mediterranean style buildings—and a feeling of humility washing over me coupled with a sense of duty, not only to those previous recruits who had gone on to protect and serve the city of Los Angeles but also to my family for its unwavering support.

Back at the turn of the 1900's, when no formal training was given to new police officers, if you met the requirements, you were handed your badge and service revolver and off you went to police your designated beat. As Los Angeles began its unprecedented growth into the entity we know it as today, however, there became an obvious need to train new officers, and in 1924 the first steps were taken to institute a program.

That fledgling training program was held in a classroom based in an armory on the site. It was an inauspicious start for sure, but it was soon to grow to new and impressive heights.

A year later, the Los Angeles Police Revolver and Athletic Club, a private organization, opened a pistol range there which would have a huge impact on the site in future years. 1932 saw the range used for pistol and rifle competitions in the Olympic Games.

After the games had closed, the department was given permission to move a dormitory from the Olympic Village which was situated in Baldwin Hills. A group of off-duty officers took charge of dismantling and transporting the structure to Elysian Park, where it was then reconstructed as a clubhouse. Today that structure is the academy's café and restaurant. Improvements to the complex did not stop at the clubhouse. Many more additions occurred over the years, eventually making it one of the premier and most widely recognized police training facilities in the world.

ACADEMY DAYS

From the time the first recruit class rolled out of the academy in 1936 until 1995, when an expansion program saw it gain several satellite branches throughout the city, every single recruit came through the program at Elysian Park, and that included me.

My first day was Monday, June 28, 1982. At a little before 6:00 a.m., I found myself standing at attention in the gym.

Facing us from across the dull wood floor was an instructor who looked for all the world like he wanted to chew us up and spit us out.

There were no pleasantries, no "Hi! Welcome! Take a place over there," just an abrupt "FALL IN!" from a guy who made you feel like he had an axe to grind, or should I say a room full of them.

As the minute hand on the gym clock ticked over the twelve and 6:00 a.m. became a thing of the past, a few recruits were still coming in and finding their places.

Our instructor went from appearing mildly irritated to full-on R. Lee Ermey mode.

Several of the latecomers were immediately dressed down and told that being late was a threat to their continued employment. None of us, even those who had turned up early, were left in any doubt as to what was expected of us when it came to being on time.

It would be the start of six months of hard work and training. By day I attended the academy, and by night I studied relentlessly. In those days, what didn't get drilled into you during academy time, you were expected to catch up on in your own time. With the studying, the making of perfect creases, and the oh-so-laborious task of spit-shining taking up all my free time, the job soon became number one. For six months, I was a slave to pursuing perfection.

Like military boot camp, the LAPD academy was no walk in the park. Although maybe not as severe, it was structured around a similar premise. There was no hiding in the back of the class. Being called out front and center was a constant threat. You had to be prepared to show not only how well you could follow orders but also how well you had absorbed instruction.

The first week in the academy was called "Hell Week," appropriately named after the U.S. Navy SEAL teams' most intense training segment. It is a week designed to break the will of all who attempt to suffer through it, a week filled with running, calisthenics and more running, all the while with instructors yelling and breathing down your neck. Traditionally, most dropouts occur during Hell Week, and we had our fair share of those who "just didn't show up" the next day.

The first couple of months continued to be intense, with relentless hounding by instructors. If they found a weak spot, they would be two inches from your face screaming abuse and, quite often, personal insults to test your resolve. More than once we were told, "If you can't handle it in here, you'll never handle it in the streets!"

Nobody enjoyed it, but we knew the system was designed to weed out those who did not belong, couldn't handle the stress, couldn't or wouldn't toe the line. A few more fell by the wayside, but after a couple of weeks you couldn't remember their names anymore. We started looking more like a cohesive unit and less like a bunch of startled civilians.

As in any job, but especially those based around a military or quasi-military logic, the instructors were looking not only for the weak links but also for the strong ones, those who stood out and could offer that extra little push to others. They were looking for class leaders.

As it turned out, I had been holding my own through their carefully constructed torment and was chosen to fill one of the positions, a decision I was neither happy with nor cherished. The one area I had no prior experience in was "giving orders." When I was told to direct the class from one point to another, to fall in or out, I was expected to do so with correct military precision and jargon.

With no prior military experience, my only frame of reference in carrying out this task was from watching those who held the role in other class squads sharing our training area. I was obviously a duck out of water.

As I was sitting in class one day, the door swung open and a member of the academy staff walked in and thundered out, "Caprarelli!" I leapt to my feet and, in my best military voice, responded, "YES, SIR!"

Then another name was shouted across the classroom: "Bartkowski!"

This guy was an ex-Marine, and he truly looked and sounded the part. A glance at him made me wonder just how many foxholes he had charged in his time. As he too stood and affirmed his presence, his voice, stance and demeanor reminded me of the old war movies of my childhood.

Right then I started to put two and two together. I could see what was coming.

We were led to the training office. As we stood at attention before our drill instructor and several other training officers, I was told that I was not filling the position as a class leader as had been anticipated. Bartkowski was to replace me.

After being ordered to complete a few push-ups just for good measure, we were escorted back to class. I felt sick to my stomach, a failure. It wasn't very long after, however, that I began to realize I was no longer in the spotlight and a feeling of relief quickly took over.

I fell back in the ranks and began counting the days to graduation day. With the workouts and drills becoming less intense and stressful, I began to notice more around me. This included the different television and movie crews that would use the grounds for filming every once in a while. One day, walking from the shooting range to the locker room, I crossed paths with actor William Shatner, who at that time was of *T.J. Hooker* fame. I was caught a little off guard when this star actually took the time of day to look at this skinny recruit and, with a smile on his face, say "Hi." I never would have thought thirteen years later I would become the Senior Lead Officer in his neighborhood.

ACADEMY DAYS

The academy was a challenge and an achievement, not to mention a time of being in the best shape I would ever be in. I knew back then that the rigors of training wouldn't last forever. I just had to grit my teeth and give it my best. As long as I passed the tests and didn't wash out on the physical stuff, I would have not only a secure career but one quite different from most—an adventure.

Though that period of my life was intense and stressful, I look back on it with great fondness, much to the disbelief of some of my fellow classmates with whom I later reconnected. It was as I remembered high school: I hated the homework and couldn't wait to graduate and get out into the world, but years later, I would jump at the chance to go back and do it again.

The hard work, including endless hours of spit-shining, finally paid off in December, 1982. Along with some fast and firm friends made along the way, I graduated, second in my class.

"Recruit" was a title of the past. It was now "Officer," but with a year of probation on the horizon to conquer.

CHAPTER FOUR

PROBATION

The academy was over, finished, in the rear view.

I was disappointed, as were two of my classmates, to learn that we would be rolled out to Devonshire Division (aka "Club Dev") to do our one-year probation period.

Devonshire is the patrol area in the San Fernando Valley that encompasses, among others, the neighborhoods of Northridge, Chatsworth and Granada Hills and was seen at the time as being a relatively slow area on which to cut one's eager young teeth. It was a mostly white, middle-class suburban area, with a few lower-income Hispanic areas thrown in.

I had requested a couple of more active divisions on my wish list, but I would learn that while we were not

PROBATION

in the hard-core gang trenches of South Los Angeles or the mega-wealthy multimillion-dollar streets of the Hollywood Hills, there would still be enough going on to open my eyes to what police work was all about.

I arrived at the Devonshire station on my first day and was immediately impressed with the near-new building. Most of the other stations in the city had been around for a while, which was reflected in their working conditions. Devonshire was modern, spacious and well-designed.

The locker room was vast, with many more lockers than there were officers at that time. As such, you could often find yourself alone in the room, making it feel like an empty warehouse, somewhat eerie.

The occupant of the locker next to mine, whom I seldom bumped into, was a veteran with a few years on the job. Although I tried to engage him in conversation on several occasions, I never really got much more than a muted "Hi" back. He would later make front-page news, but for all the wrong reasons.

That first day, after suiting up, I joined my two classmates or "boots," as probationers were typically called, in the roll call room.

Nervous and eager to not be late, we were the first there. We took three seats, several rows back from the front, dead center in the room.

A little later, several old-timers entered, made their way to the very last row of seats and deposited themselves into the wooden chairs. "Are you boots?" one of them coughed gruffly in our direction.

How obvious was it? Oh, pretty obvious: highly shined leather, creases you could shave with and stubble for a haircut. Yeah, we were boots, and they knew it.

"Up front!" There you go, the day hadn't even started and we were given our first lesson.

From then on, it was twelve months of sitting in the front row during roll call, an unwritten rule for boots. I guess they wanted you there so you didn't miss a thing; it was good logic, but the benefits of the occasional paper wad aimed at the back of your head escaped me.

Probation was a year, twelve months in which new officers, under the supervision of a succession of training officers (T.O.'s), were under scrutiny, assessed and evaluated on all aspects of practical police work.

My first T.O., "Mitch," looked and sounded a lot like a "good ole boy" who should be riding a combine harvester somewhere in Montana. He was a stocky white guy, and I could just imagine a cowboy hat on his head and boots on his feet as he fed his horses. He was an old-timer, and twenty-plus years of working entirely on street patrol had, for one thing, started to turn his light brown hair a little thin and a little grey.

Straight out of the gate, he began testing me.

We were assigned to morning watch, 11:30 p.m. to 8:15 a.m. That first night after roll call, we took our turn at the equipment room or "kit room," were assigned our radios, shotguns and police car or "shop" for the night, and headed for the parking lot. As we were approaching our car, Mitch threw the keys to me and said, "You drive." We rolled out of the parking lot just after midnight, with me receiving a short lecture about how, "Working the street, we don't take any crap."

With the brief lesson over, he said, "Wake me up if you start to get into anything" and laid his head back on the headrest of his seat and closed his eyes.

I had heard stories about sleeping on duty, and I wanted no part of it. I couldn't say anything, though. I was just a boot, and I didn't want to get fingered as a problem. My heart was racing, and I hadn't even been assigned my first radio call yet.

In desperation I thought, "Well, I'm not sleeping, so it's okay. We'll get assigned a radio call soon anyway."

I soon realized, however, as it was "Club Dev" and the middle of the night, radio calls were few and far between. The streets were empty as far as the eye could see. Nothing was going on, so I just drove, and drove, pushing our black-and-white through the streetlight-infused night.

As it was my first day on the job, I didn't know how to look for "bad guys." Unless I saw someone breaking into a car or a mugging going down right in front of me, I really had no idea what I was supposed to be doing,

I hadn't yet learned how to "dig," or recognize the subtle nuances of the street, like the body language of someone walking briskly through the neighborhood. Did he just burst out of a backyard after burglarizing a house, or was he simply late for work?

My foot stayed on the gas pedal, and the circuitous miles rolled under the tires.

As I was thinking that nothing was going to happen, that the whole city was asleep, a motorcycle rounded a corner in front of me without stopping for a stop sign. I had observed my first traffic violation.

The police car, and my heart rate, accelerated. I needed to get close enough to initiate a traffic stop and issue a citation to this "criminal." Before I could do so, however, the rider noticed my approach, made a couple quick turns and was gone. At about the same time, I noticed that my *Starsky and Hutch* driving had gotten the attention of my now-alert training officer, and as I slowed the police car to a stop mid-block in an almost pitch-black industrial area, he asked, "What do you got?"

"A motorcycle!" I replied.

With that as my only reply, he instantly knew the scenario, and giving me the feeling he was thinking, "What? That's it?" he asked me, "What's our location?"

There came that sick feeling. I didn't know.

One of the cardinal rules of working the streets is to know where you are at all times. In my excitement, I had broken this rule. I had no idea where we were. I had been too intent on chasing down my prey to pay attention to street signs.

With a reproachful look on his face that said, "Not good, kid," he took the radio mic and broadcast our exact location and that we had lost a traffic violator in the area.

Besides being embarrassed for screwing up, I was amazed at how the person next to me could know exactly where we were. He had been sleeping, and from where I had stopped, you could barely see a few parked cars alongside the barren walls of the warehouses that dominated the darkness. This cop knew his area, though.

For the duration of our assignment together, he never did lay his head back on that headrest again. I would later realize it was a test, one that I guess I half passed.

That was Day One and already two lessons, one easy and one knuckle-bitingly embarrassing, which is sometimes the best way to learn.

After my shift ended, I was still all wound up. On my first morning home, with my wife already off to work and the kids at the baby-sitter's, there was nobody to tell about my first night on the job. It would have to wait. I might have gotten a few hours of sleep that day.

When everybody got home that night and was preparing to settle in with some snacks and television, I was preparing to go back to work. It was a scenario that some cops liked, but for me it got old very quickly and became a specific watch assignment I would try to dodge throughout my career.

For now, though, it was still a new adventure, and during the next three months Mitch taught me the beginning basics of being a street cop: how to drive, where to park, how to stand, what to say. It was all pretty much geared toward the most important goal, staying safe and going home at end of watch. Getting the job done was important, but officer safety came before anything else. I remember him telling me that when it came to making decisions about our safety, "It would be better to be judged by twelve than carried by six."

How true...the wisdom of a veteran street copper. With my mental chalkboard practically blank when it came to police smarts, that mentality really stuck with me. It was the most important, and later appreciated, part of the education I got from Mitch.

After a couple months, I was assigned to another T.O. "Carl" had a little less time on the job than Mitch, but he was just as wise and adept at his own favorite areas of police work. He had a rather different personality, one more quiet and sarcastic. It gave me a "looking down at you" feeling. Trying to learn the streets was hard enough, but adding that attitude to the mix would come to tax my stress management skills.

Immediately after roll call, when all the other guys rushed to the kit room to jockey for the newer police cars to drive on their beats, Carl and I, at his instruction, always hung back. I think he enjoyed watching me fidget out of the corner of his eye as all decent rides got snapped up. As he took his time, we would routinely end up last in line, which meant the dregs when it came to what we spent the next eight hours driving around in.

Carl had ulterior motives, though. He preferred the older, smaller cruisers with "rabbit ears," those with just two red lights on top like the old *Dragnet* cars. These often heavily worn cars possessed an interior that smelled like a thousand cigarettes and spilled cups of coffee had passed through them. They were the old workhorses, each with its own lengthy history, but that did not impress me. After all, who would want a Honda when there's a Ferrari in the lot?

Sometimes Carl would even specifically ask for one of these clunkers. One night I mustered the courage to ask him why he preferred the older cars. He said they were good "alley crawlers." The newer, bigger cars were too conspicuous. The alley crawlers could weasel their way into tighter spaces and sneak around unnoticed a lot better than more recent models. The closer you could get before springing into action, the better. It made sense as far as police work goes, but I still wanted a newer ride.

Carl was a somewhat gruff and sarcastic character. There were times when he would point out my mistakes in such a way that the word "jerk" rang quietly through my mind. Above all, though, he was a good cop, and liking your T.O. was not a prerequisite to learning police work.

Among Carl's idiosyncrasies, the one that stood out to me was his obvious aversion to radio calls. Right out of roll call, he would try to get involved in anything he could so as to avoid them.

Carl had preferred areas of law enforcement. To him, real police work was about finding and arresting bad guys, not refereeing family disputes, telling neighbors to turn down their radios or taking crime reports about graffiti on walls.

At that time in my career, his attitude kind of made sense to me: I wanted to catch bad guys too. I was fresh out of the gate and eager to get involved.

As time went on, however, I would learn that police work was all-encompassing. It wasn't just about catching bad guys. It was being a mediator, a problem solver, a helper in so many different areas of people's lives. For the time being, though, Carl was the boss, and it was all about catching bad guys.

One night, deep into the graveyard shift, we observed a guy briskly riding his bike on the sidewalk away from a business strip mall area. Carl told me he wanted to talk to him. I thought to myself, "We're not going to give this guy a ticket for riding on the sidewalk in the middle of the night, are we?"

Unbeknownst to me, my T.O. was thinking about a series of business burglaries plaguing the area, and his instincts, which far outshone mine, were telling him to take a closer look at this midnight cyclist.

We approached, and the guy slowed to a stop. Carl politely asked him to get off the bike and what his name was. Remaining there with the bike between his legs and hands firmly gripping the handlebars, he disgustedly asked, "What for? Did I do something wrong?"

Carl asked him again, and again the man refused, stating those often-used words that criminals utter when the firm hand of the law drops on their surprised shoulders: "I didn't do anything."

The impasse continued, with Carl and the guy eyeballing each other. To my thinking, the situation could go only one of two ways: Either he complied, or he was removed from his bike by us. Option number one was preferred.

PROBATION

A heartbeat passed.

Thinking that this obstinate bicyclist was going to stand his ground and things were going to get ugly fast, I saw Carl do something I thought was reserved only for the movies: He took out his police radio and asked the dispatcher to send a supervisor and an ambulance to our location.

As a quick and quizzical look spread across the guy's face, he asked, "What's that for?" Carl told him he was going to have to explain to his sergeant why we had to send someone to the hospital.

With a worried look on his face, the guy got off the bike and said, "There's no need for that."

Carl radioed in and cancelled the request. He later told me that, in actuality, he had never pressed the broadcast key of the radio either time; it was just a ploy, a trick to avoid getting your uniform dirty.

We had reasonable cause to detain the guy and talk to him: He was 'fleeing' a business area during closed hours that had been experiencing a string of burglaries. Had he stuck to his mistaken thought that he was within his rights not to comply, we would have been within the law to use whatever force was reasonable and necessary to detain him.

A firm grip on the shoulder would have probably been the start, then a wristlock or armlock if he resisted, followed by the proper succession of tools on our gun belts had he made it necessary. His common sense prevailed, however—a little later than most, I'd have to say, but soon enough for me and Carl to not have to spend the extra few dollars at the cleaners.

It turned out that the guy was not our burglar. We did arrest him for some narcotics he had in his pocket though— the real reason that he was hesitant to cooperate in the beginning. Carl's instincts were right and a fine example of trusting your gut.

My gut would be tested quite soon after, but in an entirely different fashion.

Carl and I were patrolling one of the busier areas of the division, a lower-income Hispanic area that was known for drinking-in-public violations, fighting and some narcotics activity. It was around 2 a.m., and we observed a male standing on the sidewalk staring at us as we drove by.

Two things are quite common when someone does that: He is either some type of lookout and is now caught like a deer in the headlights, or he's had too much to drink and is not really sure of what he's looking at. Either way, it was a person we should have a conversation with.

Just as we exited the police vehicle and approached this now-obvious drunk, a woman came running from around the side of a nearby apartment building, screaming in broken English, "He's killing him! He's killing him!"

After taking a brief second to verify what she was saying and where she was referring to, we ran to the area she had come from and found ourselves in almost complete darkness near the rear of the apartment complex.

PROBATION

With our flashlights illuminating the way, we came upon a body, lying face up. Well, kind of face up, for the spectacle that greeted us was a male who had been savagely attacked with what we could only guess to be a large knife or machete.

The body had no face.

There were signs that the man had tried to defend himself, or at least ward off the blows that had rained down on him. Both arms lay alongside the torso but were attached to the body by only a few small pieces of skin.

It appeared that whoever had attacked this guy did so in such a frenzy that when the victim collapsed to the ground, he continued hacking into the victim's face and skull, pieces of which were strewn all around. The area looked like a scene right out of a Wes Craven movie.

Neither of us needed a biology degree to realize that there was no need to ask the person if he was okay or to check for any breathing or pulse. This guy was definitely not going to be getting up any time soon.

Following the protocol now initiated, Carl placed me in charge of guarding the crime scene, more specifically the body, and a long night became more and more surreal. It would be many hours before the coroner arrived.

I remember at one point chasing a cat away from the body, its dissipating heat quietly steaming into the cold night air. The invading feline seemed intent on snagging a free meal for itself. It was enough to make you shudder.

When the coroner finally showed up to collect the remains, he busied himself picking up the hunks of flesh and bone shards that surrounded the body and placing them in the victim's hollowed out, concave skull for temporary storage. It reminded me of when I was a kid watching my mother place decoratively carved pieces of cantaloupe back into its cleaned out half.

Hours later, after the detectives were through, evidence collected, body removed and fire department "wash down" completed, we left, as did the still-hungry cat. To this day, I have no idea if a suspect was ever arrested in the case.

Dealing with tragic circumstances as a police officer, even as a fireman or paramedic, is unavoidable. It goes with the territory.

What they don't tell you, though, what you are not taught in manuals or shown in training videos is that sometimes it stays with you. Sometimes the more traumatic events that you see or experience become a part of you and get laser-etched into your memory until your dying day. That guy with no face was one of the first.

What they also don't tell you is that these etchings can pile up. I liken it to a gas tank. Everyone who comes on the job starts with an empty tank. As you go through your career, gas (etchings) begins to fill the tank. For some, the tank never gets close to becoming full. For others, it fills fast. It's just the luck of the draw. The problem is that if you don't realize when your tank is full and beginning to spill over and don't do something about it, bad things can happen—careers, lives, even whole lives can explode.

PROBATION

Another "etching" would be the first death notification I was ever assigned.

At times, when no other avenue exists, police officers are the first to tell an immediate family member that a loved one had passed away. It is an unenviable task.

It was late one evening as Carl and I walked up to the front door of a typical single-family residence and knocked. A woman who appeared to be in her late forties answered the door, greeting us with a smile on her face and a polite "Hello." A second later, her husband appeared next to her with a relaxed but somewhat concerned look on his face. Carl asked if we could come in. She agreed, and the husband's expression now changed from concern to one of worry and even fear.

Carl verified who we were talking to and then told them that their daughter had passed away the night before, not from some natural cause or traffic accident but by suicide—the absolute worst possible news a parent could fear to receive.

I watched as those two peoples' lives shattered and crashed to the floor, never to be the same again. The mother screamed and clasped her hands over her mouth, while the father yelled "NO!" his knees giving out as he crumpled to the floor, crying.

We were to learn that their daughter had called them the previous night and had spent some time chatting, both parents blissfully unaware of what was to follow. Through the tears, the father slowly connected the dots and said to his wife, "She was saying good-bye."It was terrible.

We were there a total of about ten minutes, offering them our assistance and referral information. I was somewhat relieved to leave the house. I felt sadness for the couple's loss and thought of my young family at home. I couldn't bear to imagine receiving that dreaded knock on the door with a message like the one we had delivered.

Afterward, I couldn't disconnect. The whole scenario just stuck in my head, refusing to be shaken loose. I felt I was the bearer of bad news, a solemn portent of ruin. It was a lonely and melancholy feeling.

There were other death notifications during my career, but that first one sticks in my mind like a barbed fish hook. It will always be there. I sometimes wonder if the parents of that young woman ever learned to deal with the grief of that tragic loss.

During these early years, the radio calls that anchored in my memory didn't always involve adrenaline-pumping situations, witnessing of tragic human loss or horrific images. Late one night, we responded to one of those Code 30's, the burglar alarm calls that, the vast majority of times, are false. It was at a smaller department store, just the type of location where a manager or closing employee typically doesn't secure a door correctly and any slight breeze sets off the alarm.

When we pulled into the parking lot, it was a sea of empty spaces. We looked through the wall of glass at the front of the store, its interior dimly lit after hours. With everything appearing normal so far, we got out of our car, and I approached the store's front doors to check them. I thought there was a chance that one would pop open when I pulled on it, but they were both locked tight.

Before heading to check the back doors, I made a more careful scan, peering through the glass at the interior. It was dead calm, void of the normal hustle and bustle of shoppers, with the mannequins eerily standing out as the only "people" present.

I was just getting ready to turn and head toward the rear of the store when a movement inside caught the corner of my eye. Looking back in and upward at the store's high ceiling, I now realized what had set off the alarm. A skylight had been broken out and a rope dropped through it.

The rope was anchored on the roof at one end, while the other end was tied around the waist of a ski-masked and gloved intruder dangling fifteen feet from the floor and the same distance from his lofty escape route. It was my first cat burglar. Burglars are rarely caught in the act; let alone hanging from a rope in traditional garb. It was a Kodak moment.

When the burglar realized that I had discovered his presence, he resumed what must have been an already time-consuming and still-futile effort to pull himself back up through the skylight. Rappelling down was one thing, but he obviously didn't realize the effort it would take to climb back up. After a few minutes of struggling, then hearing the police helicopter now circling above, he decided the jig was up and lowered himself to the floor. It took a few more minutes for the store manager to arrive and unlock the door, and our high-flying burglar was off to jail.

As the weeks and months ticked by and my street education continued, something most odd would stop me dead in my tracks, this time not in the streets but in the station.

I had seen dead bodies, and I had given families heartbreaking news. I'd gotten a taste of handling the situations, seeing the sights, and hearing the sounds that the average person would never experience. Yet it was to be the sight of police evidence seals, and the place they were affixed, that would send my mind spinning.

As I approached my locker one evening to suit up for work, there they were, prominently displayed sealing off the locker to the direct left of my own. My first thought was that it was a station prank, some officers getting payback on a buddy. Something in me, though, was whispering that was not the case: It was too neat, too official looking to be a prank.

The locker's resident was the aloof cop who rarely said "Hi" whenever we crossed paths, and even that was from out of the side of his mouth. My mind reeled with possibilities: What was going on? What had he done?

I had always thought that his detachment was due to him being an old-timer and me being a probationer. There was an obvious social hierarchy within the department when it came to new recruits; we were the low guys on the totem pole. I was a boot and he knew nothing about me. I just thought he was being aloof because I was new. As it turned out, he had a lot more on his mind.

My locker room neighbor, Robert Von Villas, along with another officer who worked the division, Richard Ford, were active criminals who were later convicted of numerous crimes, including murder. These were cops? I couldn't believe it. Both were sentenced to life in state prison without the possibility of parole. Years later, looking at court records of their alleged deeds, it still strikes me as spooky that I had shared locker room space with these guys.

Rogue cops are not the norm and are in fact quite rare, despite what TV shows would have you believe. Los Angeles, however, like any major city, has had its share of corruption and greed involving those who were sworn to protect and serve

Back on the beat, the lessons continued to flow. I gradually learned the streets, the tricks that criminals use, the regular faces—all the things you would expect a rookie to be learning. Carl was a good mentor, although I may not have fully appreciated that fact at the time.

His proclivity for being obnoxious sometimes rose to the forefront. One time the word "jerk" came to mind was when I was sitting in the report-writing room, close to completing the arrest report on a drunk driver we had just booked.

I had written a couple of these before, thought I had it pretty well down pat and was anticipating impressing my T.O. I was writing the last paragraph when Carl walked in.

The room was filled with "motor cops." Until then I only knew them as the motorcycle-riding, asphalt-hardened, "give no breaks" ticket writers with bugs in their teeth who took advantage of every opportunity to have a laugh at the expense of some rookie.

Carl said, "Let me see what you got." I proudly handed the report to him. He read, at least I think he read, about half and said, "What's this?" Now every motor cop in the room was looking at me. I could feel all eyes on me, waiting in absolute perfect silence to see what would happen to the new guy.

Carl disgustedly mentioned something that he thought should have been included, ripped the report in half, dropped it in the wastebasket, said "Start over" and walked out.

For a split second I was frozen in a room where you could hear a pin drop. When I heard one low chuckle come from one of the motor cops, I internally hunched my shoulders in anticipation of an onslaught of wisecracks from the group.

Surprisingly, not a word was said and everyone went back to their report writing. These guys weren't interested in adding to my embarrassment. It got me to thinking that motor cops had hearts after all, or at least this bunch did.

To this day I'm still not sure why Carl did that. In the beginning I thought it was to impress the motor cops with his ability to "ride a boot," but I later came to believe it was a teaching exercise, though not the type I would ever recommend or eventually use myself. From then on, I was much more thorough in my report writing.

I later learned that Carl had a reputation with the other probationers in the division as being a "hard-ass." That was good for me to hear; I wasn't the only one catching his flak. It was a good day when I was eventually assigned to my next T.O.

PROBATION

About twenty years later, I crossed paths with Carl in a restaurant near where we lived. He had been retired for quite some time. He still had that sarcastic old-timer personality, but during the short time we reminisced, the old label of "jerk" I'd affixed to him never entered my mind and now seemed somewhat unjustified even back in the day. Having walked the proverbial mile in his shoes, I was actually glad to have worked with the guy.

As my probation progressed, I was assigned to work with younger training officers.

One was "Paul," who had about eight years on the job and was "cool." He didn't treat you like a boot. He treated you like a friend, a guy you could go fishing with. I was much more relaxed working with him, which on one occasion might have been a little too relaxed.

One morning as I was backing our police car into a parking spot at the restaurant where we were going to take "Code-7" (break to eat), I hit a short metal pole that was not visible in the rearview mirror. It was a tremendous thud, at least to me, big enough to cause several patrons in the restaurant to look out to see what happened.

I thought to myself, "Great! I crashed the police car. I'm on probation. I'm fired."

We got out and Paul bent down and surveyed the damage, which was a surprisingly small dent. Correct procedure at that point was to call for a supervisor and document the incident, probably resulting in a day off without pay for being involved in a preventable traffic accident.

Paul casually stood up, gave me a quick glance, said "Let's eat" and headed for the restaurant door. Quickly following, I got a couple of hard stares from some of our onlookers, who didn't seem so anxious to let bygones be bygones. When the waitress came to take our order, mine was simple: "Nothing." My stomach was so tied in knots, I wouldn't have been able to swallow a thing. For the next forty-five minutes while Paul ate, he couldn't help but flash a few silent grins across the table.

It took a few days to realize that nothing was going to happen and relax. Though it wasn't a big deal, I felt like I had dodged a bullet, a feeling that would return in more real terms in the future.

We handled many calls over the next couple of months, and Paul showed me how you could have a sense of humor and actually enjoy the job.

Late one night, we were running through a park chasing some teenagers who had caught our attention smoking marijuana and were trying to run from apprehension. Paul was whooping like an Indian chasing a herd of buffalo.

The fleeing group must have thought, "These cops are crazy!" It sure made the chase more fun, not to mention longer, which I think is just what Paul wanted.

Imagine for a second being a bystander to that particular scene. There you are, walking through the park one quiet evening, and suddenly a group of confused, red-eyed teens come barreling through the trees being chased by two cops, one of whom is uttering a Sioux war cry. You'd think it was a scene of the Village People gone mad.

PROBATION

Feeling at ease with Paul, I asked how he thought all the seasoned guys would react if I grew a mustache. I had shaved mine off for academy training, and it was an unwritten rule that you did not grow it back until you had "earned it" (whatever that meant) or you were off probation. He kind of snickered when I asked and said, "Don't worry about those guys." I guess I had earned it.

Working with Paul was a positive experience. He was a good person who showed me a personality in police work, given my limited experience, that was new to me. He didn't have an old-timer demeanor and approach that tended to be more focused on favorite enforcement activities. He welcomed everything with a "bring it on" kind of attitude.

The less stressful feeling I had while working with Paul carried over to my off-hours too. I began to realize that enjoyment of the job was formed more by who your partner was than what the job was, so it started to seem like it didn't matter what you handled. With a good partner, it was fun.

Paul and I responded to a family dispute call one night. Upon arrival, we noticed a woman in her early thirties standing in the front yard of a single-family residence. As we exited our police car, she ran up and began to frantically tell us that she had gotten into an argument with her teenage son, who was inside the house. He had locked her out and wouldn't let her back in.

The situation itself was rather mundane except for how she was dressed. She was a rather attractive woman clad only in some very skimpy lingerie. It seemed more like we were in some strip club doing a bar check than on a public sidewalk.

In her frantic state, the woman obviously had no qualms about her attire. After rattling off her story to us, she noticed a side window to her home was open and took off toward it. She pulled the screen off and tried to pull herself up, without success. With shouts that could be heard over the 80's heavy-metal music blaring from inside, she began to desperately ask us for help: "Give me a boost! Give me a boost!"

Given the hurried chain of events unfolding before us, and after a quick look at Paul to verify that we were on the same page, we decided to help and took positions on each side of her. Using the palms our hands, we pushed her up into the open window. Once she was inside, her presence was quickly discovered by the son. For a second, it seemed as though he was going to get back into it with his mother, but upon seeing our presence outside, he offered no interference when his mom went and unlocked the front door so we could enter.

As no crime was involved, we settled the dispute with a good scolding and warning to the son. For an unpredictable and often-dangerous "family dispute" call, it wasn't such a bad one to handle, if you get my drift.

Not all teenagers we came across limited themselves to smoking marijuana or locking their parents out of the house. A few weeks later, we responded to a call where the mother was not so lucky.

The detectives had already been at the location for a while, and we were called to transport a suspect to the station. When we arrived, a full-blown homicide scene was in effect. A middle-aged mother and her young teenage daughter had been shot. The mother had expired, and her daughter was on life support at the hospital. It was shocking enough, but what blew me away was the suspect: her teenage son.

It appeared that an argument between the three escalated to the point where he retrieved a gun from somewhere in the house and shot each of them in the head. I thought to myself, "How could someone do this to his mother and sister?" It was hard to fathom. When they handed him over to us, I expected to see some street-hardened, gang member, thug-looking type with a tattoo of the devil on his neck.

I was wrong. What they gave us was a young man in his early teens who reminded me of the young son on *Father Knows Best*, the popular TV show from the 60's. He was clean cut and looked more like he should be going up to receive an honor student award than being led to our police car in handcuffs. He wasn't even old enough to drive yet. It was a lesson in stereotypical thinking.

On the way to the station, looking at this young man, I couldn't help but ponder what lay ahead for someone whose life had just been ruined at such a young age.

Remember those public safety commercials, especially about fire safety, the ones that hardly anyone pays attention to when they come on TV? I can tell you they are important, accurate and not to be dismissed lightly.

We received a call late one night about a fire at a home with a body discovered inside. When we responded, amid a street crowded with emergency vehicles, water hoses and rubberneckers, you could tell that the smoke and steam of a tragedy drifted among us.

The body inside the house was badly charred but determined to be a female. It appeared that the fire had started when the woman fell asleep on her couch while holding a lit cigarette.

It was a morbid scene, with one leg bent rigidly out to the side. As the coroner and a couple of boot firefighters were trying to get the body to fit on the gurney for transportation, the bent leg snapped, sounding just like a chicken leg being pulled from the side of a fried chicken. My stomach rolled.

When I got home that morning, I undressed at the door, immediately put my uniform clothes in a bag and headed straight for the shower. The dry cleaners would take care of the uniform, but even after the shower, it would take a couple of days to lose the smell that permeated my nostrils. Months would pass before I could enjoy eating poultry again.

As a police officer, you are exposed to other people's lives on a daily basis and usually only the bad parts. Getting the skimpy underwear-clad lady through her window was a fairly lighthearted experience, but more often than not the tasks that we had to carry out were far from pleasant.

PROBATION

Here I was, on a rotating day-and-night basis, getting sent to family disputes, death notifications, neighbor disputes, home burglaries, rape incidents, assaults, shootings and on and on—all the bad stuff that's going on twenty-four hours a day, seven days a week.

Coming from an average, squared-away, middle-class family in an average, middle-class, relatively crime-free neighborhood, this exposure was a culture shock for me. Behind the scenes of what the average person sees and thinks of as regular, normal, everyday life is a whole new reality of what is actually going on in society.

It changed how I looked at the big picture. The fact was that I could no longer afford to carry the old carefree ideology of "Everybody you pass on the street is basically like you." It was now, "That person could be just like that guy who killed his parents we arrested last week." That loss of innocence began to add stress to the daily weight I carried.

The things I had witnessed and experienced in just my first year out on the street, was it what I had expected— the adventure, the variety, the chance to do something constructive? Somewhat.

I had only seen the tip of the iceberg, however. My transfer to Hollywood Division was just a few days away and would be a continuing education. Before that would occur, however, there was one more adventure to wade through before packing my bags and leaving "the Valley."

While that loss of innocence was a path that I walked right from Day One, it was soon to be driven home like a golden railroad spike. In a night of eggs and a car chase, I was to join a new club, one that brought with it a concrete realization that life as a police officer was a world unlike anything the average person experiences.

CHAPTER FIVE

EGG TOSS

It had been a little over a year and a half since I nervously walked into the Devonshire station roll call room to begin my first shift as a Los Angeles police officer. Usually, upon completing probation, you get "wheeled" to another division of assignment within a month or two. I remained in the division another nine months, often getting assigned to work with my academy classmate, Randy.

As a whole, they were good times, but the curtain was falling on my time in "Club Dev"; I was being wheeled to Hollywood Division. Though just a short hop over the Santa Monica Mountains, it was a world apart from Valley life.

Before I left the Valley, though, fate was to throw one more surprise at me, a surprise that most officers don't experience in a whole career, let alone with his wife at his side.

It was Saturday, September 8, 1984. Lynn and I decided to head out to Malibu, to Moonshadows, a cozy little beachside restaurant. With balconies jutting over the waves of the Pacific Ocean, it was the perfect setting to chow down on my favorite fare, seafood. We would be joined there by Randy and his wife to celebrate our transfers to Hollywood Division.

As the night wore on, Randy and I took to reminiscing about the academy, what each of our probation trials had been like, and some of the more interesting busts we had made while working together.

It was an enjoyable night, and around 11:30 p.m., after contentedly stuffing ourselves on seafood and happy recollections, we said our good-byes and headed in opposite directions.

With Lynn at the wheel of our fairly new Oldsmobile, we started up the winding Kanan Dume Road back through the mountainous canyons toward the San Fernando Valley. As we were talking about our conversations with Randy and his wife, I thought about how difficult the past two years had been on Lynn and our marriage.

We had gone from practically being joined at the hip to barely seeing each other. From day one, she was supportive of my career change, assisting me with studying and keeping the military creases in my uniforms during academy training, all the while holding down her own job, caring for our two-year-old, John, and being pregnant with our second son, Jimmy.

Once I hit the streets, she found herself alone most nights and weekends, functioning as a single parent and worrying about me. Although I shared a lot of my experiences with her, to protect her innocence I kept most of them to myself.

Many times Lynn would awaken at 3:00 a.m. to find my side of the bed empty when I should have been home by midnight. Fearing that something had happened, she would sometimes pace the floor and eventually call the station to make sure I was alright.

She confided to me years later that during those early years, before going to bed, she routinely had her hair and makeup ready to go in case she got that knock at the door from some of my colleagues with that dreaded news. I felt bad that we hadn't talked about her fears at the time, but she had been concerned that if I knew how afraid she was, it would have caused more stress than I was already experiencing.

She was probably right. I knew many of the guys whose wives whined and complained about their careers. It was definitely not something they looked forward to going home to after a long shift. Lynn was devoted to making my off-hours time that I could relax and enjoy, whether it was at home with my family or out with friends like this evening.

After about thirty minutes of chatting, we merged onto the straighter path of the eastbound Ventura Freeway and, with only the quiet hum of the tires to be heard, I told Lynn, "I think I'll take a little snooze." Just as I laid my head back in the headrest, a loud smash from the back of the car engulfed the interior. Something had hit our rear window.

As I turned to look, a dark green Toyota cruised up along Lynn's side of the car. Its occupants were two middle-aged looking men, both laughing. The passenger held up an open egg carton for us to see. Several eggs were missing, and it didn't take a genius to figure out what had happened.

I thought to myself, "You don't know who you're messing with." A lesson was to be learned and class starts now.

I retrieved my LAPD badge and held it up for the two juvenile-minded pranksters to see. Even though Lynn's window was closed, the freeway lights and distinct profile of the badge would have made it unmistakable as to what I was displaying at them.

In apparent slow motion, two things happened next: The proud grin melted from the passenger's face and the egg carton fell from view, both immediately replaced by a rather challenging look and the brandishing of a large-caliber (.357) blue steel revolver. The driver wasn't as bold, however, and the Toyota raced ahead of us, remaining just within range so that I could still see the passenger holding his gun in the open window.

They say that "hindsight is 20/20." Looking back now, at that point in the situation with my wife driving the car and no such thing as a cell phone to call for assistance, a cooler, wiser head would have let their car fade into the distance as we continued home and called in a report later. That's easy to say now, but back then, as I was still somewhat a rookie cop and gung-ho, my mind instantly went into "work mode." A crime had been committed, and I had to at least get their license plate number.

EGG TOSS

I told Lynn, "Follow them!" and we began zigzagging through the sparse late-night traffic in an attempt to close the gap between us. Just after turning southbound on the San Diego Freeway, the driver decided to ratchet things up a notch and made an abrupt turn off the freeway. We were now heading onto surface streets.

With barely a flicker from the Toyota's brake lights, it continued onto the dark, quiet and tree-lined streets of the surrounding neighborhood.

At the first intersection it came to, the Toyota's taillights flared brightly as the driver stomped on the brakes and brought the car to a screeching halt. Lynn had to swerve our car quickly around it to avoid a collision, bringing it to a stop turned slightly in front of their now-stationary vehicle. Bathed in the headlights of their car, I felt like a sitting duck.

So much for just getting the license plate number now.

Instinctively, I swung the door open and found myself standing with my badge held up in my left hand and my right down at my side clutching my off-duty five-shot Smith and Wesson revolver.

The engine of their car immediately began to race. Thinking at any second that I could be road kill, I raised my gun, pointed it at the driver and yelled, "Police! Stop!"

Instead of lurching forward, their car began to creep backward, turning its tail slowly to the left and bringing the still-open passenger window into full view. Again, I yelled, "Police! Stop!"

They did, just long enough for the driver to shift into first and put the pedal to the metal, causing the rear tires to start spinning. At the same time, the passenger yelled something to me—to this day, I don't know what—and raised his handgun again. There was no intent to brandish it this time. In a split second, from fifteen feet away, he pointed the gun at me and pulled the trigger. The muzzle blast and flash momentarily eclipsed the squealing, smoking tires of their car.

The single .357 round raced past, inches away from my outstretched left arm, leaving stinging fragments in my skin. Continuing another eight feet, it found a home in the open passenger door of our car. Penetrating the interior panel, it nicked the bottom of the closed window, causing it to shatter.

My mind was on autopilot now, and survival mode kicked in. I fired three rounds from my gun. All three missed not only the dirtbag who had just tried to kill me but the entire car as well (further verifying the challenges regarding accuracy when using a two-inch-barrel handgun in a combat situation).

Their car was now moving behind our car and to the driver's side, Lynn's side! Was she the next target! I took a quick step forward and, looking at the back of their car, had to make my last two rounds count. I squeezed off the first round, which penetrated the passenger side trunk area of their car. I squeezed off the second, my last round, which penetrated the driver's side trunk area. Two hits! That got their attention, and with no return fire, the Toyota—now with an air-conditioned trunk—raced away, disappearing into the night.

EGG TOSS

It was suddenly eerily quiet. The smell of gunpowder hung in the air. Looking back at our car, I saw Lynn's head slowly appear above the front seat. Panic set in: "You okay!" Though her voice was a bit shaky, her response was music to my ears: "Yeah, what about you?" The fact that I was at least still standing was good enough for me to reply "Yes." I looked down at my stinging arm. Small dark spots, some with signs of oozing blood, peppered the back of my left forearm. Though it didn't really sink in at the time, six inches to my right and the hit would have been center body and end of story.

Looking back up, I noticed lights coming on in the nearby houses and residents beginning to peer out their windows. The front door of the house nearest me opened, and a bathrobed gentleman stepped out hesitantly to see what all the commotion was about. I yelled, "Excuse me!" Caught a little off guard, he froze, looking at me. I said, "I'm a police officer. Call 911, tell them I was just in a shooting and need assistance." With a nervous sigh of relief in his voice, he said "Okay" and scurried back inside.

My adrenaline still pumping, I walked back to our car. I was going to sit down until I noticed all the glass fragments. They littered the ground as well as the front seat. Some clung to Lynn's hair. As I leaned against the fender to wait, I began to realize just how fortunate we were. I could tell that Lynn was all pumped up. Being at the wheel during a pursuit that ends in a shooting is enough to get even a seasoned copper's adrenaline going. It was an experience that would later give her a better understanding of the times that I would come home still geared up myself.

As we waited for assistance, I began to worry. What if those guys decided to return and get even for the bodywork I had done to their car or, for all I knew at that point, to themselves? A wave of relief accompanied the arrival of the first two uniformed officers. Though only six minutes had elapsed from the first call until the officers arrived, it seemed like an eternity. They immediately put out a broadcast describing the suspects and secured the scene. Detectives, Scientific Investigation Division personnel and a supervisor were requested. The first supervisor to respond was from Devonshire and, as luck would have it, was greatly admired by street coppers. He'd been an excellent street cop himself as well as a supervisor and led me through the monotonous on-scene investigation that followed.

While still at the scene, we were informed that the two egg-turned-lead throwers had been taken into custody at the Van Nuys Police Station. I said to myself, "Wow! That's quick police work!"—or so I thought. They hadn't been observed and chased down by fellow officers. They had driven home, hidden the gun under a mattress and concocted a story to cover the presence of two bullet holes and (from a couple of prior poorly tossed eggs) copious amounts of egg yolk on their car. Then they went to the police station to file a report.

The egg would end up on their faces instead. About halfway through their desperate story of being assaulted with eggs and shot at while driving, the report taking abruptly ended. The officers at the desk, having earlier heard the original crime broadcast about the incident, put two and two together and immediately handcuffed both of them. The two very surprised visitors were now long-term guests at "the Gray Bar Hotel."

Later that night, which was now beginning to see morning light, I also paid a visit to the Van Nuys station to wrap up with the detectives, and though the injuries to my arm were quite superficial, procedure dictated that I have it looked at by the doctor in the jail dispensary. Passing through the jail, I walked by the bench where arrestees are handcuffed while waiting to be processed. As is usually the case, several were sitting there waiting with their heads hung low, except for one.

A rather large guest was not looking toward the floor like the others. With eyes revealing a hint of fear and bugging out of his head, he was staring at me. It wasn't the first time on the streets I'd seen that look from a law breaker coming to the realization of his fate, so I took little note, but as I passed through the jail security door and it slammed shut, a realization came over me. I swung around to take another look back through the jail door window.

It was him! The dark figure in the car who just a few hours earlier had tried to plug me with a bullet was now sitting just feet away. He was still staring at me and knew I recognized him but then turned his face, heaving an apparent sigh of relief for the steel door separating us.

I got checked out and, exhausted, met back up with Lynn in the lobby of the station. We headed home, appreciating the morning sunrise just a little more.

CHAPTER SIX

HOLLYWOOD NIGHTS

Hollywood—the spiritual home of American movies, a schizophrenic realm of nonstop "lights, camera, action" and post-production parties. To the left and right of the red carpets, light shows and hoards of fans clamoring for a glimpse of their favorite stars, however, was a different world, one cast in shadow by the bright lights and hidden in the darkness, streets often dominated more by pimps and prostitutes than by sightseers and tourists. It would be an eye-opener to me and a world that I would get to know quite well.

It was a warm summer evening as I turned left off the Hollywood Freeway. Just three blocks away on Wilcox Avenue was my new assignment, Hollywood Division. Between the theaters and hotels, I could see the Capitol Records Building standing tall, watching over the eclectic crowds of people, a veritable zoo that was jamming Hollywood Boulevard.

There were lights everywhere, and among the revelers, general street traffic and all the shenanigans in-between, the feeling of "expect anything" (or, should I say, "everything") crackled in the air like a broken neon sign. As I walked into the station, I wondered how long it would be before I got a taste of those streets.

Getting to know the neighborhood was going to have to wait a while because as a new guy in the division, and like many before me, I drew the unenviable assignment of working the station jail. That assignment was often quite boring and repetitive: Fill out paperwork, attach plastic wristband, take booking photo and escort to accommodations for the night. Throw in an occasional burrito distribution, and that was it—your typical work schedule.

It was the same thing over and over, night after night. I was itching to get out and explore the streets. I felt this job should belong to an old-timer, someone six months away from retirement, someone who wanted to cruise out the last few months of his tour in relative peace and quiet.

Luckily, I didn't have to wait too long. After only two months, I got a change thanks to my old buddy Randy. He had gotten himself assigned to the Prostitution Enforcement Detail in the station's vice unit and had arranged a way for us to work together.

The PED unit, as it is called, was formed just prior to the 1984 Summer Olympic Games to focus on the more-visible aspects of the prostitution activity and its related crimes occurring on Hollywood's busy streets.

The unit consisted of ten to twelve uniformed officers in unmarked police cars who would scour the streets. Any presence by prostitutes was given "full attention" according to the law. That covered everything from throwing a gum wrapper on the sidewalk to lewd conduct in public. Our goal was to disrupt their trade and make it no longer cost-effective for them to do business in the area.

During the day, with the area mostly left to the tourists and non-prostitution-related crimes, the PED Unit ran only a skeleton crew. The bulk of the unit worked at night, 6:00 p.m. to 2:30 a.m. You've heard the saying, "The freaks come out at night"? It was pretty much true, and Randy and I found ourselves right in the thick of it.

Cruising the streets of Hollywood on a nightly basis was like having your own first-class season ticket to the circus freak show tent, front row seats no less. The "ladies of the night" came in all shapes and sizes—and, well, they weren't always ladies, if you know what I mean. There were a few times it took a closer look to determine if we were going be booking at the women's jail or heading to the men's. In time, however, I learned to tell from a mile away.

A lot of the time, we played a game of cat-and-mouse. When we observed someone we knew was trying to ply the trade but committing no obvious criminal violation for which to issue a citation, we would keep out of view and quietly follow and watch our unsuspecting entrepreneur until a customer, or "John," showed up and struck a deal. Sometimes the wait was only minutes long, other times an hour or more.

Motels were not used much by street prostitutes. Rooms cost money and took much more time to complete the deal. Business was usually conducted in an alley, in the client's car or sometimes right there on the sidewalk. Each scenario was often within spitting distance of the usually unaware public.

That's where we came in. Trying not to draw the attention of any other public presence or passersby in the area, we would approach our streetwalker/customer combo as stealthily as possible as they were still in the process of consummating their deal.

With a subtle tap on the shoulder or car window and an unmistakable announcement of our presence and profession, startled responses were quite the norm. Right there, in that moment, anything could happen, but for the most part embarrassment and compliance ruled. If there were no extenuating circumstances or surprises, a citation for lewd conduct in public was issued rather quickly, and we were off looking for our next "collar."

That was our main job night after night, week after week, month after month. After about six months, Randy left PED to work another specialized detail, something I should have tried following him into, but I continued with prostitution enforcement, teaming up with a couple of other good partners.

In addition to springing surprises on streetwalkers, we came across occasional drug and weapons violations arrests. We also got to work with Hollywood Division's main vice unit. This usually involved manning one of the chase cars during prostitution stings.

They would place an undercover female police officer, subtly dressed for the part and wired with a mic, out on the street to just "hang out." When a John would come by and proposition her, we would swoop in and make an arrest for solicitation of prostitution.

It was surprising the cross section of society that got caught up in that situation. It wasn't just the proverbial businessman on a long trip succumbing to the wild side. Over time, I saw people from all walks of life; clergymen, well-known actors, firemen, and even policemen joined the list. One night, my partner said that the guy we just booked was one of his old high school teachers. It seemed no one could be ruled out of getting caught in the net.

When I wasn't searching for lewd conduct violations or manning a chase car, I was put out in an undercover car myself, wired with a mic, to approach prostitutes and see if they would proposition me. Not all were women, either. We also had to give attention to those areas where men plied the trade.

Some of those conversations, if not so perverted, would have been almost comical to me. It was a tricky task, as most of the more seasoned prostitutes were adept at playing word games when trying to arrange a deal. If they didn't offer sex for money, there was no crime, and if you pushed too hard for that offer, they would sense you were a cop and be "in the wind." At times, it took some talent, something Hollywood has always demanded for any kind of success. When you did obtain a violation, you would drive the car to a predetermined location nearby where your partner was waiting, announce yourselves and make the arrest.

Not everyone was a street-hardened prostitute, and every once in a while I would come across someone who would play no word games. Usually nervous and sometimes embarrassed, they would cross the line right into a violation rather quickly. When the jig was up and they realized their predicament, they would often burst into tears and start begging us to let them go. They weren't seasoned prostitute "lifers" or drug addicts but women so desperate to buy food for their kids that they would resort to selling themselves.

This began to weigh on me. I never felt that what they were doing was justified, but bearing witness to their desperate choices to earn a dollar, and then throwing them in jail, started making me feel sorry for them. I pictured hungry young hatchlings in their nest eagerly waiting for their mother to come home, not knowing that her wings had been clipped and she would not arrive anytime soon. It was a Catch-22 situation. Prostitution fueled other crimes and in no way benefited the long-term practitioner. I knew that, but at times I couldn't shake the feeling that, for some, I was making things worse. It left a sour taste in my mouth. I was getting too involved.

That's when I knew I had to move on. The PED unit and I had run our course together; it was time to leave, not just the PED unit but Hollywood Division itself.

I began to eye a transfer to North Hollywood Division, back to the Valley and closer to home. Shortly after putting in a request, I received an invitation to work a short-term loan with the Central Bureau Undercover Narcotics Buy Team. It would be an interesting change of pace and a different level of street experience to obtain before shipping out to the Valley, so I jumped at the chance.

I didn't realize it at the time, but it would be like jumping from the frying pan into the fire.

For a couple of weeks, I worked on looking like a dope addict, a user. I grew my hair longer; I couldn't bear to part with the mustache, so I extended its real estate and grew out a scruffy goatee. With the addition of some oversized clothes to make me look as if I had lost weight from drug use, I was almost ready to go. The finishing touch was a narcotics detective's talent in using pencil lead and eraser to make some pretty convincing needle tracks and scars on my arms. I fit the look rather well and was ready to go buy dope.

I'm not sure how happy my wife was in greeting what looked like a dirtbag junkie home every night, but duty called and it wouldn't be forever.

The Narco Buy Team's day would start with a morning meeting with the detectives at Parker Center. Our intelligence briefing was akin to those typically seen on TV. Information regarding where dealers were hanging out selling dope was obtained via a network of street scouts and other undercover officers and then passed on to us. For the most part, our targets were wary and street smart, with an uncanny ability to smell a cop. We just had to be smarter. We had to toss aside the cop presence, the cop smell, and make them feel comfortable enough to swap some cash for a little "weed" or "blow."

With our target areas delineated, we would roll out. In a nondescript rental car, gun tucked under my leg, police radio switched off and hidden under the seat, I would cruise looking for those obviously out to help me "score."

We weren't usually outfitted with mics when buying dope. Drug dealers were a little more thorough than prostitutes when it came to looking for signs of a cop. It wasn't surprising.

Most vice violations were misdemeanors, while most drug violations, including sales, were felonies. Long-term prison sentences were much more likely, which made attempts to flee more common and a whole lot more dangerous.

There were many times you knew that the dealer, who was inches from your open window or sometimes even in your passenger seat, was armed, not as much for a confrontation with the police but to protect themselves from other drug dealers who might try to take their product or attempt to displace them from already claimed turf. Real estate is coveted in the drug world, and if someone tries to remove someone from ownership, they couldn't exactly call a cop for protection.

We were like a Trojan Horse in the middle of it all, looking to be brought in close enough to enable springing of the trap. Sometimes it took a steady nerve.

UNIFORM DECISIONS

I would drive by the designated locations looking like a scraggy white boy addict, eyes bugging out of his head and desperately seeking a fix.

The type of drug and dealer that we went after depended on the scout reports. If we were going for marijuana, when a potential dealer looked at me, I would press my index finger and thumb together and hold them to my lips, imitating smoking a roach. If it was cocaine or some other nostril candy, I would brush my thumb alongside the side of my nose.

It was as simple as that to initiate contact, a subtle movement mostly missed by anyone around except those who knew what to look for. If the dealer had what I was asking for, a slight nod would be my invitation. Sometimes I wouldn't even have to give a sign. I'd simply drive down the street and dealers would be flashing the signs to me, in essence saying, "We got what you want."

With that we were in; the invitation to buy had been laid out, and now came the tricky part.

Transactions usually passed off smoothly. A dealer would talk until he felt sure you weren't a cop. This ranged anywhere from a fast glance and greeting through the car window to a conversation a few minutes long with the person sitting in the seat next to you. When they felt comfortable, business could commence.

A quick flurry of hand movements and money went one way and a small baggie or foil wrap came back the other. Then the dealer melted back into the street traffic. With my part of the job completed, I would drive away from the location, appearing to be another happy customer. Once clear, I would retrieve my radio and notify the chase cars that a buy had occurred and provide a description of the suspect. I was done, but for the chase cars it was just the start. Suspects inevitably ran for it. Nine out of ten times, it was the same: a futile attempt often ending with some sort of altercation.

There was one time during my tour, however, that a suspect decided to shoot at the pursuing officers, a sharp reminder of what the people I was coming in contact with were capable of. It was just what I thought I'd come across one night while trying to buy some cocaine.

At 8:30 p.m., on a street just north of Hollywood Boulevard, I spied a middle-aged African American guy hanging out around the entrance to a seedy motel. The word was that he was dealing cocaine, so when he tossed me a glance, I brushed the side of my nostril and he made his approach.

After a quick look inside my car, he opened the passenger door and got inside—a bold move before any words had been spoken. I took my foot off the brake and began to creep down the street.

I have no idea what set him off. Maybe it was the fact that we were moving away from his turf, or maybe he saw something that I had missed, but before I knew it, he freaked out and yelled, "STOP THE CAR, STOP THE CAR!"

Trying to maintain composure, calm this guy down and still get him to sell me some drugs, I said, "Take it easy. You got any coke?"

Whatever was going on with this guy, he wasn't in the mood to tell me, and definitely not going to sell me any drugs. With no answer to my question, he grabbed the steering wheel with his left hand and continued yelling, "STOP THE CAR!"

It was all moving very quickly. I wanted to ask what the problem was, wanted to calm him down and still make a buy, but that was obviously out the window.

In a quick glance away from trying to maintain control of the car, I noticed that he was wild-eyed with his demand and had slid his right hand underneath the left side of his jacket.

"GUN!" rang through my mind, the adrenaline notching higher; this situation was starting to tilt way out of control. If he had a weapon under his jacket, he wouldn't even need to pull it out. He could fire through his jacket and the bullet would slam into my unprotected right side from just eighteen inches away.

The time had come to give him what he wanted. I threw the car to the curb and pressed hard on the brakes. In a flash, his door flew open and he was gone, the door bouncing gently on its hinges as I watched a receding pair of heels flee into the night.

I let the chase cars know what had occurred; no buy, but something was definitely up. They chased him down and caught him holding some cocaine, but no gun. It was no consolation to me. It still felt like I had a very close call.

I liked undercover work; there was a "spice" to it, a flavor you couldn't taste in any other area of police work. It had its shelf life, though. Just like the wanted posters for criminals that we had on the walls of the police station, drug dealers kept mental posters of cops posing as buyers. Getting positively identified as a cop on the streets trying to buy drugs was an ineffective if not dangerous position to be in.

After a pit stop back in the PED unit, my transfer to North Hollywood Division came through. It was back to the Valley in a black-and-white.

I liked working street patrol, a radio car. Even with the exposure to all the negatives, if you had a partner you enjoyed working with, it was actually fun most of the time.

As a Police Officer 2, or P-2, I would find myself working the desk or the jail every once in awhile, but a typical year would be months of working with a partner, cruising the streets looking for bad guys, somewhat like a shark in the water.

Unbeknownst to everyone, elsewhere in the Valley a quiet criminal friendship was in its infancy, a friendship that would eventually prove to be a destructive meeting of minds and would one day alter so many people's lives.

The clock was ticking down. No one could have foreseen what was coming to North Hollywood.

CHAPTER SEVEN

MOVING UP THE LADDER

A typical day on patrol usually produced a sight or activity that I hadn't seen or done yet, but after thousands of radio calls and hundreds of arrests, a lot of the work started to seem like an assembly line. Everything pretty much fell into basic categories: Family disputes would be handled in one of three ways, burglar alarms in one of two ways, narcotic arrests one way and shoplifters yet another way.

You couldn't let your guard down, though, because within the hours of tedium, sporadic seconds of gut-crushing, heart-racing adrenaline inevitably popped up. If you weren't always on your toes, you could easily end up on your back.

Traffic stops were one of those daily activities that you could find yourself getting very lax in handling when it came to officer safety. I routinely reminded myself of the scenarios in which officers had made mistakes and lost their lives in the process of issuing a citation. I tried to treat each stop as though anything could happen. It was a good mind-set to have and something I wished an old-timer I was working with one day had practiced.

We saw a red light violation and pulled the car over. It was midday in a business district on one of the busier boulevards, with lots of cars and people around. I got out of the driver's side of our cruiser and slowly approached the driver's side of the car as my partner approached the passenger side just ahead of me. He took a quick look inside and gave the signal that it was okay to approach. Through the driver's window I saw two teenage girls sitting in the front seats. Things seemed pretty innocuous, enough so that I noticed my twenty-plus-year veteran partner decide to "relax."

He took his eyes off monitoring the girls and turned around, apparently to gaze at the fine weather we were having that day. "C'mon, guy! Let's do this by the book" flashed through my mind just before I asked the driver for her license and registration. As she began to dig in the purse next to her, she asked the passenger to look in the glove compartment for the registration.

I was now splitting my attention between the purse and the glove compartment. Before the driver could produce her license, out of the corner of my eye I saw the passenger grab what appeared to be a small, two-inch-barrel .38 caliber revolver that had tumbled from the open glove compartment.

In a flash, my mind processed the situation: My partner was standing just a few feet away with his back facing someone holding a gun, and she had the drop on him if she wanted to take it. With the whole scenario taking no more than four or five seconds to develop, I drew my weapon as I took a half step back and yelled "Gun!" to alert my partner.

At this point, I realized my finger had slid off the frame of my gun and was resting on the trigger, an action almost always followed by a round being fired off. The passenger looked at me and froze, still holding the gun. My partner spun around, and I heard him utter a surprised "What?" As he looked at me, not in the car, I kept my attention on the girl. Another disgusted "C'mon, guy!" flashed through my mind.

He turned his attention back inside the car and finally grasped the situation. He quickly reached in and took the gun from the girl. It turned out that the "gun" was actually a starter pistol left in the car by the driver's brother, a track-and-field enthusiast.

Though not much was said between us, I could tell that my partner was embarrassed and knew that I was pissed off. Had he kept his attention on the task at hand, he probably would have recognized that what tumbled into the girl's hands was only a starter pistol. If not, he still could have grabbed it much sooner and avoided the situation reaching the point where a few ounces of finger pressure would have made a very ugly scene.

Even following all the rules and procedures, having the best tactics doesn't nullify the fact that, in some circumstances, if the bad guy wants to take you out, he can. That's where instincts come into play. They help level the playing field. Working the streets long enough results in some uncanny calls as a result of instincts, or a cop's "hunch."

One evening, during another traffic violation stop, I told my partner that we should "call this guy out." This meant that instead of approaching the car, we would ask the driver to step out and direct him to the curb to make our contact.

I wasn't sure exactly why I decided to change the usual procedure on this particular stop. Did it take a second or two too long for him to pull over? Was it the darkness of the area or the isolation of the freeway on-ramp we were on? Nothing by itself really stood out, but my instincts were screaming "Something's up."

Our cars rolled to a stop. From behind the door, I yelled to the driver, asking if he could step out of his car. There was no response or movement for a few seconds, so I yelled the request again. After a couple more seconds, he got out of his car, at which time I directed him to walk to the curb where my partner was now standing.

As he complied, I walked up to the driver's side of his car and did a quick check for passengers. No one was inside, but what caught my eye raised the hair on the back of my neck. On the driver's floorboard, lying on its side, was a black steel, 9mm semiautomatic handgun, positioned as though the last resident of the seat had been holding it between his legs and decided to drop it before getting out of the car. It had one bullet in the chamber and a fully loaded clip.

We couldn't pin any other crime on the guy and ended up booking him for possession of a loaded firearm— surprisingly, under certain circumstances such as this, only a misdemeanor in California. He obviously wouldn't cop out to anything, especially why the handgun was there, but I just knew that if I had walked up to the window of his car, I would have been a sitting duck. There were many times, though not all as potentially lethal as this one, that paying attention to instincts kept things from getting nasty.

After a few years of "hookin' and bookin'" as a basic street cop, I decided to promote to P-3, Training Officer. With nearly eight years on the job, most of it working patrol, I was feeling very comfortable on the street. It was time to pass on what I had learned to the newer officers who were just getting their feet wet. The bump in pay was a welcome benefit too.

It was a jolt from what I was used to, not a large one but definitely a change. Working with a seasoned partner was usually a smooth operation. We knew tactics, procedures, how to write reports, and we took care of each other. After a while, you could practically read the other guy's mind. Working with probationers right out of the academy was a whole new ball game. The only thing they had down pat was spit-shining their leather.

Reflecting back to my time as a boot, I tried to piece together all the good qualities of the training officers I had worked with and form them into my own particular brand of teaching.

Patience was one of the first things to spring to mind. I didn't want to come across as a sarcastic jerk like a few T.O.'s I had experienced early in my career. Probationers sometimes needed ongoing and repeated instruction in report writing and certain other procedural areas. That was no big deal, but when it came to officer safety, I couldn't have cared less if I seemed like a jerk or not. All the academy and accumulating field training had better be put into practice. There was no room for persistent lapses in that area. To let poor officer safety practices continue was akin to playing Russian roulette with five of the six chambers loaded. It wasn't really a question of whether the gun was going to fire but when and how many people might get hurt.

Training new police officers was rewarding. Not only did I feel like I had a positive role in the all-important formative years of officers' careers but their zeal and desire to learn often rubbed off, taking me back to my own early days on the job. It kept things fresh. That's not to say that there was no added stress. Sometimes I felt like a baby-sitter, which led me to cut a little more slack when remembering some of my past training officers.

So for a few years I trained probationers, teaming with a succession of newbies to answer radio call after radio call. The "etchings," those calls that would remain a negative memory to carry forever, continued to accumulate, and they weren't all related to bad guys and close calls.

There was the family dispute between the alcoholic parents of a four-year-old boy who clutched my leg and with desperate, tearful eyes begged me to take him with me when we left.

Especially gut-wrenching was the time we had to remove two young sisters from their home. While we were handling a dispute between their parents, the mother accused the father of abusing the children—falsely, I believed. It wasn't for us to decide, however, and the die had been cast. We had to place the girls, only five and seven years of age, into the temporary custody of the Department of Children Services until the agency and our Juvenile Detectives could figure out if anything had happened and whether it was safe to return them.

As we led the girls to our police car, we did our best to explain what was going on, but it had no affect on the amount of tears flowing from their eyes. It was the middle of the night, and the only foster care available was downtown. We were to meet the social worker at Southwest Division to hand over the kids. On the way, the girls became more relaxed and trusted us that "everything will be okay." Stopping to buy them ice cream also helped. By the time we arrived at Southwest station, they both seemed as if they could have been with some favorite uncles taking a trip to the park.

Things quickly changed, however, when we got out of the car and walked into the station. The lobby displayed its years of heavy use, and several citizens inside were arguing about something. The expression on the girls' faces quickly turned to fear. Though they didn't fully understand what was happening, they were certain of one thing: They didn't want to be there.

A disheveled-looking man, cigarette dangling from his mouth and wearing a suit he had obviously slept in, approached us and identified himself as the social worker who would take them to where they would stay. When the girls realized we were handing them over to this guy, the tears started flowing again. They begged to stay with us. We tried again to assure them that everything was going to be okay, but to no avail.

As we left, the girls were still crying, their two little faces looking at us as if to say, "Why are you doing this? We trusted you." It tore at my heart. Making it worse was the possibility of them being separated from each other in different foster care locations. Even though removing the girls from their home was in their long-term interest and the right thing to do, I felt like I had let them down, that in their eyes I was the bad guy who had tricked them. Not knowing how things turned out for them haunts me to this day.

Peppered throughout the montage of a patrol officer's duties is the handling of "welfare checks." These calls for service have nothing to do with low-income households or government subsidies. They are calls from people, usually relatives or neighbors, who are concerned about the well-being of someone who hasn't been seen or heard from for an extended period of time. Our job was to try to establish contact with the person, make sure they were alright and ask them to get in touch with their concerned family member or friend. Usually it was a situation where phone service was interrupted, an extended vacation had been taken or the person had moved. A simple phone call by either them or us remedied the situation.

Sometimes, however, the person had passed away, sometimes under circumstances not so ordinary. Over the years, I came across quite an array, from the guy who decided to take a plugged-in toaster with him into the bathtub to the woman who tied a rope around the bathroom doorknob, draped it over the top of the door and hanged herself on the other side.

Not all were suicides, however. One afternoon, my partner and I responded to a house where the owner had not been seen or heard from for several weeks. When knocking on the front door resulted in no response, we began walking around the residence looking in the windows as we made our way to the backyard. Everything seemed rather normal except for one thing. The windows I checked each had an unusual number of flies crawling on the inside of the glass. With a few years' experience under my belt, I instantly knew what this pointed to. Making our way to the back door, we found it locked with a familiar odor of death seeping around its frame. With a little effort, we made our way inside, the full force of the odor confirming our suspicions. Now it was only about locating the body.

The house was pretty much sealed up with no lights on inside, making it rather dark, and, being midday, we didn't have our flashlights in hand. Making my way to the bedroom, I looked through the doorway and saw a figure, obviously deceased, lying in bed. It appeared to be a natural death. Besides the now-overwhelming odor, something else stood out. The body was lying on its back and its eye sockets seemed to be moving. In the dim light, I couldn't figure out what it was, but this didn't look like any corpse I had seen before.

We went back outside, called the coroner's office and waited for their arrival. When we all went back inside and opened up the place for some air and sunlight, I discovered what the movement was. Because the body had been decomposing for quite a while, maggots had formed colonies over each eye socket and were busy carrying on their business.

That wasn't my only surprise. Waiting for the coroner's deputy to complete her investigation, I noticed some odd spots on my uniform sleeves and shirt. They looked somewhat like the pollen specks left behind when you come into contact with a blossoming flower or honeybee. There weren't any flowers or bees in the house, however, only flies, and an abundance of them. It didn't take an entomologist to figure out that the spots were being caused by the flies first landing on the dead body in the room and then paying a quick visit to us.

One other experience on this call would be new to me. When it was time to remove the body, it had "melted" into the bedsheets and had to be peeled away, kind of like removing a Band-Aid from a scratch a little too early.

As shocking as this all was, it wouldn't be this welfare check that threw me for the biggest loop. Another one, under somewhat similar circumstances, would take that prize. This time, there was also no answer at the door. Checking windows, I caught an obscured view of what appeared to be an elderly woman of slight build lying almost facedown on the kitchen floor of her older and noticeably unkempt home. I advised my partner of the situation, and we gained entry through a back door.

Although the signature odor of death wasn't there, the interior smelled as if it hadn't been exposed to fresh air for weeks. I made my way to the kitchen. On the floor was the woman, lying there for who-knows-how-long. A couple of feet from her, I bent down at the knees, half to see if there was any preliminary evidence of foul play and half to ponder what the last moments of this woman's life must have been like.

I was caught completely off guard when she quickly rose up on both arms and lifted her head to face me, an expression scrawled across her face that seemed to say, "What do you want?" Outwardly I was frozen in my squatting position, but inside my heart skipped a beat before a rush of adrenaline put it in fast-forward. After a second or two of all those zombie and vampire movies I saw as a kid getting their two cents' worth, I called to my partner to request an ambulance and then tended to the woman.

She could barely communicate, but I was able to determine that it was one of those cases of "I've fallen and I can't get up." Within about fifteen minutes, the woman was on her way to the hospital for a checkup. This was my first "come back to life" incident, and it put a whole new twist on future welfare checks that I would handle.

A few years went by, and the shine of training probationers began to fade. Add to that the constant exposure to all the negatives associated with working a radio car, and my stress level increased. Like so many others I had worked with, I began cracking open a few beers at end of watch to relax, to escape. It became a routine.

Uniformed patrol always included a fair share of weekends every month and shift changes every five to six months. My two sons were now in their Little League years, and even with my luck in continuing to avoid the graveyard shift, working nights and most weekends was robbing me of time with them that I would later regret missing.

When an opening for promotion to P3+1, Senior Lead Officer, in North Hollywood Division came up, I jumped at it. The position was still a uniformed street assignment, but with fewer radio calls, day watch hours and only rare weekend assignments being the norm. I also got another bump in pay.

This change didn't come without a trade, however. Senior Lead Officers were also assigned to be the community liaison for one of the specific "basic car areas" in the division. The responsibilities included being the first contact for the public regarding ongoing crime problems, personal safety, neighborhood watch and other quality-of-life issues. Most of my time shifted from handling radio calls and chasing bad guys to conducting community meetings and solving problems. I became a mediator and a department face for a segment of the division.

That area was Sun Valley, a largely older, bedroom community where, other than a few gang problems, crime was relatively low. It was a good place to learn the ropes regarding community-oriented policing. I had time to get familiar with all the other city agencies involved in handling quality-of-life complaints and to hone my public speaking skills at the various meetings.

As I was settling into my new role, an incident festered to a point that it eventually caused Los Angeles to explode in a fervor of hatred. On March 3, 1991, an African American man named Rodney King, a convicted felon, took patrol officers on a high-speed chase and then resisted during his arrest. Four white officers were recorded on videotape using their batons on his arms and legs.

The media was selective in what it showed from the tape, which was played over and over again. At first glance, it appeared to be an outrageous case of police misconduct. Fractured was the trusted "thin blue line"; destroyed was our reputation as "the good guys." On April 29, 1992, a jury acquitted the officers on almost all charges. The uproar was almost immediate, within thirty minutes of the verdict becoming public. In the blink of an eye, districts of Los Angeles erupted in a frenzy of misguided looting, violence and murder.

When the insanity burnt itself out nearly a week later, the LAPD was left to wander among the vehicle wrecks and looted stores, trying to put back together communities and an image that had been severely damaged. That's the thing about being part of an organization: When something goes wrong, everyone is tarnished, in this case painted with the heavy-handed brush of "All cops are racist thugs."

It took several years of hard work to return to our previous status quo; in the meantime, a subtle tension filled the air, a feeling that the flash paper could be lit again at any moment. That in turn translated to patrol officers being a great deal more careful on the street.

Just when I had gotten comfortable in my new digs, I was reassigned to the Studio City area of the division. Studio City was a far cry from Sun Valley. My beat went from still-aging, World War II era neighborhoods with walls covered in graffiti to multi-million-dollar homes overlooking Universal City and the San Fernando Valley.

With the new real estate came more crime. The high-class restaurants and shops along Ventura Boulevard were targets for burglaries and thefts. The crowds that frequented the area tended to drive expensive cars and carry bulging wallets, which drew car thieves and more daring street robbers. At the bottom of the food chain was the ever-present and revolving chorus of homeless street beggars. Though they were small in number, their presence was visible to all and generated more complaints over the years than all the other crimes combined.

It took a while to get in the groove there, but when I did, it was like I had died and gone to heaven. Working patrol and responding to radio calls didn't allow officers the time to solve most of the complaints that citizens would have. "If it happens again, call us" was often the best that could be done. It was a frustrating line to hear from someone you were asking for help.

That's where I came in. As a Senior Lead Officer, I now had the time to follow up and coordinate everything at my disposal to end problems. Though the occasional disgruntled citizen still reminded you where your paycheck came from and demanded instant results, as a whole the frustrated faces of the past were becoming more and more faces of relief and thanks.

If the problem was midnight music routinely blaring from one of the hundreds of homes nestled in the rolling hills, I could adjust my schedule and track it down. If it was a gang of pranksters tirelessly targeting some street with vandalism and graffiti, I could stake it out and catch the offenders red-handed.

Other problems, more serious in nature, got the same attention. One was a motel complex on Ventura Boulevard experiencing an increase in thefts and narcotic activity. A note left at the station asked if I could stop by and talk to the owner about what could be done.

When I pulled my police car into the parking lot of the motel, Holly House, it seemed as if I had just driven onto the movie set of *The Grapes of Wrath*. The individual bungalows scattered around were small and overgrown with bushes and ivy, white paint peeling from the aged wooden window frames. There were no signs of any guests, just the leaves in the breeze dancing across empty parking spaces.

On a hill at the end of the property was the office; a tilted "No Vacancy" sign hung in the window with "No" half covered by a piece of cloth. Knocking on the door, I could hear the sound of creaking footsteps from within slowly approaching. When the door opened, I was caught a little off guard by who greeted me. In a sweet, grandmotherly voice, an elderly woman who might have approached five feet tall said "Hello" and invited me in.

The interior of the building seemed much larger than the exterior, and from the furnishings I could tell that this was where she not only conducted the business of the motel but also lived. My visit lasted only ten minutes, during which time she told me that she was the sole owner/operator and was having an increasing problem with tenants not paying their bills and making excessive noise coming and going in the middle of the night. There was also evidence of narcotics use left in and around rooms on the property.

My first thought was to ask why at her age—she must have been at least seventy-five years old—she was trying to run the place anyway. Because of its location, the property alone could demand a fortune, even in the condition it was in, and offer her a life of ease in retirement. That wasn't for me to figure out, however, or the proper advice to offer, so I told her that I could help.

Starting with some extra patrol by the units working the area, I began to focus some selective enforcement at the location. During and in-between the visits that I made to weed out the junkies and prostitutes who were slowly trying to claim the motel as their safe haven, I got to know more about the property itself and the woman who had made it her life.

Elaine had been there for over forty years and told me stories about the old days when vacationing families would rent rooms to spend a few days visiting the nearby studios. Some would be lucky enough to cross paths with an aspiring actor staying in the room next door for a few days to pitch his talents to those same studios. There was no visible criminal presence and very little crime at all. "Those were the days," she would say, a time that she clung onto dearly.

My continued efforts over the next two years never brought back to that motel the look and feel it once had; criminal elements were always waiting in the wings, but Elaine didn't know or care. As long as she had that policeman, John Caprarelli—whom she even named her cat after—watching over her, she felt as if things were just fine, just like the good old days.

Her failing health finally demanded the sale of the property and her move to a senior care facility. I visited her a couple of times as she slipped into a new reality, one from the past in which she didn't recognize me anymore. It seemed like a good ending. At least she hadn't been left to the wolves and in constant fear of street hoodlums knocking on her door those last few years.

This was a different type of police work, and very rewarding, but it didn't compare to slapping the cuffs on a criminal you had just chased down. The dinners at home every night made it worthwhile, though, and my wife was happy, too. I wasn't coming home every day with the latest story about some pursuit, altercation or close call. There was still the occasional arrest and radio call to be handled, but to her it seemed like I now had an office job.

That would turn out to be far from the case.

Los Angeles in the 1990's had gained the unenviable, media-hyped title of "Bank Robbery Capital of the USA." It was an epidemic that was truly out of control, with as many as five robberies a day in Los Angeles County alone.

May of 1996 saw two particular crime reports circle the Valley, standing out in the fray of hundreds of others; they detailed two takeover bank robberies that had gone down within three weeks of each other, committed by the same men. The robbers had been dressed in body armor and ski masks and had brandished fully automatic AK-47's, that most iconic of all assault rifles.

I remember browsing the reports and thinking to myself, "Heaven help the officers who run into these guys." I had no way of knowing at that point that I would be front and center for a melee that would go down in history as being one of the largest urban gun battles on record.

PHOTOGRAPHS

With my parents John and Dawn, 1968

With Lynn at High School "Grad Nite" at Disneyland, 1975

UNIFORM DECISIONS

Lynn's Uncle,
LAFD Captain Chris Irons

LAPD official hiring photo
June 1982

Academy Graduation Day
December 1982

Devonshire Division Special Problems Unit, 1984

NARCO Task Force, February 86

With my wife Lynn, 1992

The annual LAPD Baker to Vegas Relay Race

PHOTOGRAPHS

Issuing a traffic citation in the early 90's

Neighborhood Watch cleanup day, 1993

UNIFORM DECISIONS

Bank of America Shootout on February 28, 1997
(photos courtesy of Gene Blevins)

PHOTOGRAPHS

Bank of America Shootout on February 28, 1997
(photos courtesy of Gene Blevins)

UNIFORM DECISIONS

One of the weapons used on February 28, 1997
and the destruction it caused

PHOTOGRAPHS

To John Caprarelli
With Appreciation,
Bill Clinton

In the Oval Office of the White House

TOP COPS Awards, Washington DC, October 1998

UNIFORM DECISIONS

With LAPD Chief Daryl Gates at the Jack Webb Awards, 1998

LAPD Medal of Valor Awards, 1998

PHOTOGRAPHS

With LAPD Chief William Bratton, 2007

Son Jim with his wife, Leah

Son John with his wife, Carolina

CHAPTER EIGHT

DAY OF DAYS: FEBRUARY 28, 1997

As the sun climbed above the San Gabriel Mountains, its weak winter rays stretched out over the roofs of the San Fernando Valley, crawling through alleyways, filtering through the tree-lined streets, brushing away the pre-dawn shadows. An unprecedented day in Los Angeles history was coming to light.

In a nondescript house in the Valley community of Granada Hills, two men were making final preparations for their day at work, two men with twisted and violent dreams, who had robbed and killed before, who by the time this day was over would gain international notoriety.

Thirty miles northwest of Granada Hills, I was awake and preparing for my own day, my morning ritual the same as millions of others that Friday morning: shower, breakfast with the paper, kiss my wife good-bye and head out for the "office." Fridays typically involved thoughts of weekend chores and activities. This particular Friday was no different, with not even an inkling of what this fateful shift had in store for me.

In the interior gloom of that house on Ludlow Street, Larry Eugene Phillips, Jr., and Stefan Emilian Decebal Matasareanu worked quietly, gathering their work tools and sorting their clothing. Phillips, the perceived ringleader of the two, was a dominant personality coupled with an acidic hostility for police. That huge chip on his shoulder made for a very dangerous character. Before the sun would set, I would witness and experience the fruits of that hostility.

Twenty-six-year-old Phillips was a native Angeleno. He also had close family ties in Denver, Colorado, having both lived and been arrested there some years previously. He was a 5'10", 196-pound, gun-loving bodybuilder of Mexican and Italian descent who some say was a master of disguise. Having several well-worked identities and seemingly able to switch between them at will, he was a ticking time bomb. His life had been littered with small criminal arrests, mostly property fraud, and with each arrest it seems the spring within him became wound a little tighter. One day, that spring was bound to snap and violently uncoil. Today would be that day.

His partner in crime and reported best friend, Emil Matasareanu, was a thirty-year-old, 6'2", 300-pound bear of a guy. A naturalized Romanian immigrant, he had lived most of his life with his mother in the family home in

Altadena that also doubled as a care home for mentally disabled adults. Since childhood, he had problems integrating into the California way of life. He made many friends but appeared to be unable to keep them for long. Those who had crossed his path later recalled him to be a jovial, good-natured and friendly person. Buried not so deep under that sociable veneer, however, was an anger born of years of childhood bullying, family dysfunction and current pressures of a failing business. His one true friend, Larry Phillips, had not been wisely chosen.

After a chance 1989 meeting in a branch of Gold's Gym, they became firm friends. From Matasareanu's standpoint, the friendship offered everything he craved: social acceptance, a long-term friend, a kindred spirit who could understand his inner rage and share his passion for firearms and computers. For Phillips, the friendship grew into something darker over the next three years. When his own dreams started to crumble due to poor life choices, he saw in Matasareanu a willing accomplice who would follow him into some murky depths, including the criminal underworld. It turned out that Emil had the guns and Larry had the plan.

It is widely believed that the duo's criminal enterprises started in 1993 with a rather unsophisticated robbery of a Wells Fargo armored truck in Littleton, Colorado. Two men matching the physical descriptions of Phillips and Matasareanu, dusted with theatrical makeup, charged their target with a rifle and handgun and escaped with just $23,000.

Later that year, Phillips and Matasareanu were stopped in Glendale, California, by an undercover auto theft officer while carrying a trunk full of ammunition. That wouldn't have been too bad except that along with the 2,000 rounds, they also had four pistols and two semiautomatic AK-47 clones. Add into the mix ski masks, body armor, smoke grenades and a police scanner, and police and prosecutors saw a virtual bank robbery kit. Due to a plea bargain, however, minimal sentences were handed down and both men served less than three months. Soon they were out of jail and planning their next caper.

Then they appear to have gone quiet for a considerable time. Shortly after Phillips' release from jail, his mother, with whom he had a very close bond, passed away. Maybe this flung him completely into the abyss. We will never know.

We do know that in June of 1995, the pair resurfaced in a particularly brutal and senseless crime. At the rear of a Bank of America in Winnetka, while midday traffic flowed by mere feet away, they attempted to recreate their Littleton robbery. Only this time instead of rushing the guard, they shot him from a close distance and then went in after the money. Fifty-one-year-old Herman Cook was hit three times in the chest and died several hours later. He never even had a chance to draw his sidearm to defend himself. He left behind a grieving widow, two teenage children and a community and police force shocked by the level of violence.

At the cost of a man's life, Phillips and Matasareanu had escaped with $122,500. The reward money offered for their crime turned out to be more than the amount they had stolen.

1996 saw their downward spiral intensify. Their first job was an attempt at stopping a moving armored car by firing an AK-47 at its driver from their own moving vehicle. The plan ended in disaster. After only wounding the driver, who escaped, the duo ran for their safe house, leaving their burned van and equipment in a nearby alleyway.

Apparently honing the skills of their trade, they changed tactics and hit the big time by targeting banks. Two takeover robberies in May of 1996 saw them net close to $1.6 million. They didn't bother with bank tellers, notes or subtlety. They simply stormed the banks dressed in body armor and ski masks and went straight for the vault.

Most noticeable, however, was they had now graduated to fully automatic weapons, and had the propensity to use them. The FBI bank squad gave them a name: "The High Incident Bandits."

In late February of 1997, on quiet, tree-lined Ludlow Street, both men now moved to prepare for their fateful day. If all went well, they would be home by 10 a.m. high on adrenaline and hundreds of thousands of dollars richer. They were already sitting on a small fortune, but greed overruled their common sense.

Patiently waiting in the driveway of the single-story house that they occupied was a nondescript, white 1987 Chevrolet Celebrity, its windows tinted, insignias removed and displaying a license plate stolen two months earlier from, astonishingly, a Van Nuys LAPD officer's personal car. The trunk of the vehicle remained ajar, the spare wheel well lined with a blue bath towel. In it were contained, among other accessories, box and drum magazines for AK-47 variant rifles, 100-round Beta-C snail drums for an AR-15, and 40-round box magazines for a Heckler and Koch Model 91 (HK 91) assault rifle.

Their weapons were next into the trunk. It was a lethal arsenal: three Chinese-built Norinco Type 56's, an HK 91 and a Bushmaster XM-15. Four out of five had been illegally altered to fire as a fully automatic gun. The level of firepower was staggering, absolutely and unequivocally unwarranted for the job that they were about to tackle. The Norincos alone were easily capable of putting ten rounds a second downrange—ten rounds a second! Think about that for a moment, that amount of firepower to rob a bank. Most bank robberies were committed without a single shot being fired.

After loading the rifles into the trunk of the Celebrity, they went into the house where Matasareanu had once lived with his wife and children. Both then suited up.

Emil Matasareanu threw on his usual cream-colored bulletproof vest, supplementing it with a steel trauma plate slipped into the front. His arms and legs went unprotected.

Larry Phillips sported some extra attire, however: 43 pounds of Kevlar-type protection, which included at least five distinct vests that had been cut and fashioned to form a modern-day suit of armor. After stripping down, he wrapped the first two pieces around his thighs, pulled on his pants and wrapped the next two pieces around his shins. Velcro and black duct tape held everything together.

He then donned a light grey, long-sleeved T-shirt. Bulletproof arm wraps were put into place, after which came a full vest complete with groin guard, a bullet-resistant flap that hung down from the bottom of the vest.

An assault vest, with its many pockets stuffed full of AK-47 and Beretta 92 magazines, followed. Over the top of the assault vest, Phillips strapped on a brown leather "Miami Classic" shoulder holster made by Galco. A webbing belt with four pouches that contained 75-round drum magazines for the AK rifles circled his waist. A chromed Beretta Model 92 was nestled snugly under his left armpit. Phillips would be carrying close to 60 pounds of protection and firepower.

Each man wore a pair of black leather Hatch gloves, their usual ski masks and custom-made sunglasses, Phillips choosing a dark pair and Matasareanu sporting one with a yellow tint. Oversized windbreakers, purchased by Matasareanu via mail order from a firm in Gray, Tennessee, completed their attire.

Breakfast was to be a half dose each of Matasareanu's anti-seizure medication, phenobarbital, a strange choice of drug for soon-to-be bank robbers. Phillips also took one of his own allergy medications.

It was 8:30 a.m.

The Chevy inched off the sloped drive at the Ludlow Street address and crawled southbound, headed for North Hollywood, its passengers hidden from view behind its heavily tinted windows. Behind them, at the house, the only things moving would be dust motes until Robbery Homicide detectives turned up later looking for clues about the past occupants.

As the Chevy dipped off the drive and onto city streets, I was heading through the door of the police station. In the locker room, I changed into my uniform, my second "blue skin," making sure that my bulletproof vest was strapped down snugly under my shirt. I wasn't thinking about dodging bullets, however, just what kind of neighborhood problems might come my way.

I slid my Beretta 92F out of its holster and did a chamber check, making sure that a live round was seated inside. Then the gun was back in its holster, thumb snap secure, and I was off to the Community Relations Office.

It was 9:11 a.m.

Phillips and Matasareanu pulled the Chevy into the north parking lot of the Bank of America at 6600 Laurel Canyon Boulevard, taking the second disabled parking spot against the north wall. It was as close as they could get to the bank doors without parking on the street. Interestingly, Matasareanu parked the car facing "nose-in" to the wall. It was a curious tactic, as backing into the parking spot would have made for a much speedier getaway.

Sitting behind the dark-tinted glass, both bank robbers put on their sunglasses and ski masks, those nearby going about their daily business blissfully ignorant of what was transpiring. Phillips did a quick check on the police scanner sitting on the bench seat between himself and Matasareanu. The biggest thing on the airwaves was a commercial burglary that officers were being directed to.

"Let's Go!" Both doors of the Chevy swung open. Two monsters in black emerged and a history making event was initiated.

The Chevy remained idling, and the pair walked to the trunk as if they were unloading groceries. Nobody had spotted them yet, but that luck was only to hold for another fifteen seconds.

Matasareanu selected a Norinco rifle, complete with 75-round drum. Phillips would take an almost identical rifle, also loaded with a 75-round drum but with a large vertical foregrip designed to steady the weapon under fire.

A dozen short paces later, they had left the rear of their vehicle and were now on a walkway parallel to the bank leading to its north entrance. In full view of the morning traffic cruising by on Laurel Canyon, they strode toward what they thought would be an easy take.

That's when their luck ran out. Walking southbound on Laurel Canyon, they were momentarily slowed as they approached the ATM lobby by the presence of a customer who had just deposited a check. As Phillips grabbed the unsuspecting customer, forcing him back into the bank, North Hollywood Division Officers Loren Farrell and Martin Perello, on routine patrol cruising past the bank, stared in disbelief. It was obvious to them what was about to unfold.

Had the bandits made their move twenty seconds earlier or later, had the customer not been in the ATM lobby and impeded the pair's progress, had the cruiser been traveling 10 m.p.h. faster or slower, the robbery would have gone down like the previous two, with Phillips and Matasareanu snatching a large sum of cash and making their way back to their safe house.

A few miles away, back at the station, I was talking to another officer and getting ready to hit the streets when I heard Loren's steady but excited voice crackle over my police radio: *"15-A-43 requesting assistance, we have a possible 2-11 in progress at the Bank of America, Laurel Canyon north of Kittridge."*

Fridays between the hours of 9 and 11 a.m. is the danger window for banks. Most robberies happen during that time frame, so this one occurring when it did was not unusual. Having a bank robbery in progress observed by someone and called into the police while it is still being committed, however, is rare. The odds of having it observed by two police officers are almost astronomical. These criminals weren't going to get away.

I jumped in my police car and headed for the bank. It was only two to three minutes away. On the way, several more transmissions came over the radio, mentioning the descriptions of the suspects and that the officers didn't think the robbers knew they'd been observed. One really got my blood pumping, though: *"We have shots fired!"*

Inside the bank, customers were being thrown to the floor, the security guard also planting his face on the tile. Four single shots rang out, deafening in the enclosed space, swiftly followed by an ear-piercing volley of twelve full automatic rounds as Matasareanu moved to the armored teller door and shot the lock out. The air inside the bank quickly filled with panic and gun smoke.

Then over the radio I heard, *"Officer needs help!"* My foot pressed down on the gas pedal a little harder.

The "North Hollywood Shootout" had begun.

CHAPTER NINE

OFFICER DOWN!

It was now 9:18 a.m.

"DOWN! DOWN! EVERYBODY ON THE FLOOR! THIS IS A ROBBERY!"

Four single shots rang out, the 7.62x39mm casings spitting from the side of the rifle and clinking to the floor. Hardly a breath passed and Matasareanu moved several steps to the left, striking a seventy-nine-year-old customer with a backhanded blow to the head, knocking her to the floor. Raising his rifle amid the screams and shouts of surprise, he took careful aim and squeezed the trigger. Twelve bullets left the muzzle in a little under a second and a half, shattering the polycarbonate around the lock of the teller lines' "bullet-resistant" door. A muffled panic now pressed those cringing and yet undiscovered even deeper in their hiding spots. Those lying on the floor did their best to remain still and not draw any attention.

Outside, the noise from Matasareanu's rifle could be heard for quite some distance. A scattered few walking in the surrounding area paused, perhaps thinking "Gunfire? Must be filming a movie somewhere."

The interior of the bank continued to be a carefully planned and choreographed chaos. For those trapped inside, the next seven and a half minutes would seem like an eternity.

Phillips and Matasareanu stuck with their tried-and-tested plan: Phillips worked crowd control in the lobby while Matasareanu found the day gate keys and ransacked the vault. There were a few small differences from their previous robberies, however. Matasareanu did not touch anything within the vault and instead directed the assistant manager to load the duffle bag, and Phillips left the teller drawers and money alone, perhaps to pay more attention to their captive audience.

The level of violence was pushed to a higher level than in earlier heists. Gunfire was not just about breaching the teller door. It was now used as further intimidation. With what seemed a much more aggravated temper than during their past robberies, Phillips fired shots into the ceiling.

As Matasareanu ripped open the broken teller door and stormed through the teller line. Phillips needlessly bent down and punched an already-prone customer in the face. Turning, he then jammed the hot muzzle of his rifle into the security guard's neck as he lay on the ground, telling him that on command he was to move all the customers to the vault. Shakily, and under Phillips' threats to execute him if he did not comply, the guard nodded his head.

Control was complete, but for some reason Phillips was not yet satisfied. He strode around the lobby calling for the "pig," the "undercover," to show himself. It was a strange action, one possibly pointing to increasing paranoia about law enforcement closing in on their criminal behavior. Phillips raised his rifle and fired off more shots, the atmosphere in the bank now seeming to reach almost critical.

Over the radio came another broadcast: *"There are more shots being fired inside the bank!"* As storefronts flashed past my windows, the words buzzed around in my head, "This is going to turn into a full-blown gun battle."

The situation in the bank continued to escalate. The bank's assistant manager was now being confronted by the 6'2", 300-pound, machine gun-wielding Matasareanu.

With Matasareanu ordering him to empty the steel cabinets that contained the "bricks" and "straps" of bank notes into a large black canvas bag, the assistant manager found himself in a tight spot. There was nowhere near the amount of money that the robbers had expected. The bank had altered its delivery schedule.

The black duffle bag stood between them, half filled with 40 pounds of plastic-wrapped note bundles, a total of $303,000. Tucked away among the bundles were also three dye packs.

From behind his ski mask, Matasareanu glared at the bank employee and repeatedly demanded more money. There was no more to give, and an uneasy silence settled over the vault.

Outside and 200 feet to the north of the bank, Sergeant Larry "Dean" Haynes, Unit 15-L-40, positioned his black-and-white across the southbound lanes of Laurel Canyon and proceeded to take over the direction of incoming units. Two citizens who had heard the gunfire spotted Haynes and made a beeline for his car.

Back inside the vault, the silence was broken when Matasareanu, escalating the situation to a breaking point, again demanded more money. Swinging the muzzle of his rifle upward, he fired more shots, hitting one of the cabinets inside the vault. Several shards of shrapnel wounded the terrified bank employee.

As I rounded the corner and headed north on Laurel Canyon Boulevard, I could see the bank ahead of me. Dean's cruiser, just north of the bank, was blocking the southbound lanes at Archwood Street. I slowed my police car and, a couple hundred feet south of the bank, turned the wheel so that my car partially blocked the northbound lanes just south of Kittridge Street. All appeared to be eerily quiet at that point.

A little ahead and to my left in the Hughes supermarket parking lot, I noticed a few officers stationed behind a key-cutting shack. To my right, at the southwest corner of the bank's south parking lot, I spotted a small group of officers and detectives behind a cinder block wall. Feeling exposed in the middle of the street, I left my black-and-white and made my way to the group behind the block wall.

Inside the bank, as the reverberations from the shots in the vault died away, the only other sounds to be heard were muffled prayers, muted sobs and Larry Phillips' footsteps as he strode back and forth.

Then Phillips noticed something: There was no traffic passing the bank. Slowly, he cracked open the northwest door. Seeing nothing in front of the bank, he stepped out into the ATM lobby, then a few steps further down toward the sidewalk. The scene that confronted him was deceptive. To his right, he saw Sergeant Haynes' cruiser parked across the southbound lanes. To his left, a little further away, was my cruiser blocking the northbound lanes. I don't believe he knew at that point that many additional officers were taking up positions in other locations all around him.

Without a shot being fired, he spun around and casually re-entered the bank.

Crouched by the cinder block wall near the south lot, I waited with the others. I could feel that something was building. These guys were definitely not going to walk out with their hands up. In the distance, I could hear the wail of sirens, other officers desperately trying to make their way to the bank.

Dean, having been updated by the two citizens, keyed his radio and broadcast: *"L-40, be advised. I got two witnesses here who say there's possibly two or three suspects inside the bank with possible AK-47s, wearing ski masks and dark clothing."*

The clock was ticking down. Confrontation was inevitable.

With things happening so quickly, and the area being so large, there had been insufficient time to clear the streets and nearby buildings of any civilian presence. Many people were still walking around the area. The Hughes supermarket directly across from the bank was busy with shoppers coming and going. Cars continued to make their way through openings in the still-forming police perimeter. Next door to Hughes, a group of elderly ladies chatted while under the driers in a hair salon, completely unaware of what was to soon disrupt their morning peace.

Back inside the bank, Phillips and Matasareanu were making preparations for their exit. Phillips barked at the security guard to move all the customers to the vault. Along with a female bank employee, the guard managed to usher most of the frightened group into the cramped relative safety of that small room.

As Dean stood behind his black-and-white trying to get more information from the two people who had approached him, a third witness joined his group. The twenty-eight-year-old woman had driven into the north parking lot earlier and heard gunfire from within the bank. Deciding that it was wise not to hang around, she drove to another nearby location and called 911. The operator informed her that the police were already aware of the situation. Discovering Dean and the two others standing next to his police cruiser parked nearby, she scurried to his location to tell him what she had heard.

At about the same time, rolling to a halt behind Dean's cruiser was a black-and-white containing Van Nuys

Division Officer Martin Whitfield, who took up a position behind his vehicle. This group of two officers and three civilians were seconds away from becoming Phillips' first targets.

Above them, LAPD helicopter unit Air 8 had arrived on scene. Its crew would have clear airspace for the next ten minutes; eventually, it would share that space with five media choppers and a Wessex from the Los Angeles Sheriff's office. Air 8 would become an integral part of the day, its officers remaining overhead during the entire incident relaying everything that they saw to the ground units below.

Just under seven and a half minutes had elapsed since the robbers burst through the bank's north door. With weapons far superior to those carried by patrol officers and body armor that was practically impenetrable, they apparently thought that any attempt by police to stop them would be futile. Phillips and Matasareanu would soon discover that they were indeed boxed in and that, as futile as they might have thought it seemed, we were going to try to stop them.

It was time for them to leave. With the cameras in the cash machines recording, Larry Phillips gripped the door handle with his gloved hand and threw the door open. He marched out into the open ATM lobby and immediately turned to his right, the muzzle of his Chinese assault rifle swinging rapidly up to eye level.

From only 200 feet away, the officers and civilians behind the two police vehicles parked in the street caught a glimpse of what was to come. Phillips, the monster in black, raised his rifle and targeted the group. Dean pushed the female civilian to the ground as the rest of the group headed in the same direction.

The front sight of Phillips' rifle bracketed the cruiser as his gloved finger squeezed back on the trigger.

The acoustics from those first shots were deafening. South of the bank, we instinctively ducked our heads a little deeper into our collars. Phillips continued firing, raking the two black-and-whites from stem to stern with automatic gunfire.

In less time than it takes to blink, numerous rounds tore into both cars, causing crippling damage. As they rocked on their suspensions under the repeated impacts, rounds sliced through the thin doors like they were paper, slamming into seats and ricocheting off any hard surfaces that they struck, some rounds traveling through the cars and out the other side. Tires popped and airbags went off. Had anyone been inside either car, it would have been instant death. As the three civilians huddled behind the rear wheel of Dean's car, they were showered with shattered glass and metal splinters; two wounded by rounds that had hit their mark.

The noise was indescribable: a continuing rampage of cracks and thunder booming and echoing back and forth between the buildings that lined the street.

A single fully automatic AK-47 makes a whole lot of noise, but when Matasareanu joined his cohort in the lobby, the sound of two became the stuff of nightmares. It was the devil's symphony, and something that has stayed with me even to this day.

Dean, crouched behind his car, watched as gunfire literally shredded it. Rounds ricocheted off the hood and buzzed over his head. With several missing him by inches, one struck him in the shoulder. He and Martin decided to change their location and move to some nearby trees. Not only would it be better cover, but they could draw fire away from the wounded civilians still lying huddled next to the police car.

Both took off toward the trees, instantly drawing attention from the two robbers. Shots rang out again, skipping in the street behind them and slamming into the houses in front of them. Before they reached safety, both were hit by gunfire, Dean receiving a grazing wound to his leg and Martin a much more serious wound. Faster than the speed of sound, a round smashed through his thigh, pulverizing five inches of femur in an instant. Dragging himself behind a tree, Martin would spend the next twenty-five minutes clinging to life.

Dean urgently broadcast over the radio, *"I've been hit, and another officer behind me has been wounded also."*

That opening salvo was immense and a wake-up call to anybody who hadn't figured it out yet: We were in big trouble. Compared to their firepower, we had peashooters, and the rounds were literally bouncing right off them.

Phillips, his weapon now empty, ducked back into the ATM lobby. Stripping the spent 75-round drum from his rifle and dropping it at his feet, he plucked another from the web belt around his waist and jammed it into the rifle. Racking the charging handle, he stepped forward for Round Two.

Again a booming cacophony filled the air. Using moderate bursts of gunfire this time, Phillips continued to target the two black-and-whites closest to him, some of the rounds hitting the still-huddled civilians. Their quick thoughts of running for it were abandoned for playing dead in hopes of losing the gunman's attention.

Stepping forward to rain down more terror on the stranded civilians, Phillips instead was going to get a rather heavy smack on the back.

A little over 200 feet southwest of him, on the other side of Laurel Canyon, was the small key-making shack. Using it for cover were Officers Stuart Guy and James Zboravan and Detectives Tracey Angeles and William Krulac.

Zboravan, a boot with only two months of street time under his belt, was about to inflict the first wounds on Larry Phillips. The results illustrated that Phillips would not go down easily that day.

With Phillips' attention honed in on officers in the Archwood and Laurel Canyon intersection, Zboravan slid forward the pump on the Ithaca Model 37 shotgun he was holding. Chambering a round, he slipped around the side of the key shack and lined the sights on the barrel on Phillips' back. It was a long shot to make with that type of weapon but, with a little luck, it might be effective enough to incapacitate the target instantly.

He fired a round and, slamming the pump back and forward, fired another. Two charges of heavy copper-coated buckshot streaked across Laurel Canyon, striking Phillips in the right side of his back. With most of the buckshot being absorbed by the thick Kevlar he was wearing, one pellet fell low and punched between the layers of armor, burying itself deep in his right buttock. Instead of crumpling to the sidewalk, Phillips was saved by the body armor he had so meticulously donned. Obviously agitated, he staggered momentarily and turned his attention to the shotgun-wielding officer.

Stung and enraged, Phillips opened fire on the flimsy shack. Diving back for cover as a huge salvo of gunfire ripped through the sheet metal structure, Zboravan grabbed Angeles and pinned her to the ground, putting himself and the bullet-resistant vest he was wearing between her and the fusillade of bullets now coming their way. There was no real cover, as the high-powered rounds being fired were penetrating everything. For now, it was either pure luck or divine intervention keeping them safe.

Other officers, still stationed in the south parking lot of the bank, watched in anguish as the shack was riddled with bullets. There wasn't much they could do. The direction the robbers were taking kept them out of their sights, and trying to make it to the key shack would have been suicide. In the face of superior firepower, things were going from bad to worse for us.

With the key shack being no cover whatsoever, the officers and detectives behind it had no other option; they had to move. Before making it to other cover, all would be wounded, with Zboravan, the officer gaining Phillips' attention with the shotgun, receiving two serious wounds. Traveling at 2,400 feet per second, one bullet tore across his lower back and the other hit his right hip.

"I'M HIT! I'M HIT! OFFICER DOWN AT THE BUILDER'S EMPORIUM!"

From the relative safety of our block wall, a veritable firefight was transpiring just a stone's throw away. Despite the terrifying noise from the numerous rounds being exchanged, I was able to hear all the transmissions coming over the radio clearly, including the desperate calls for help from my fellow officers. I had not yet seen either of the robbers. I had no idea what the guys causing all the panic and mayhem looked like. I did know that they were dressed in all black and obviously using some high-powered weaponry.

I couldn't just sit there and wait to see if the fight came to me. I had to do something. I had to seek these guys out, to try to stop them before anybody else was shot or they got away.

Shadowed by another officer, I left our group at the brick wall and made my way to the first street east of and directly behind the bank. As I headed north on Archwood Street, the "officer down" calls continued to stream from my radio, the desperation in the voices increasing.

The disciplined automatic gunfire showed no signs of abating, the relentless cracks and booms permeating the air as well as my memory.

Passing houses on Archwood, I came across a driveway that led to a backyard directly behind the bank. Ducking into it, I found it not only too far south for a commanding view but also separated from the bank by a high block wall.

Phillips continued to alternate his aggression between the citizens and officers pinned down just north of the bank and those in the parking lot across the street. Having made a mad dash for safety, Zboravan and Detective Krulac dove into a nearby dentist's office. Both had been shot, Zboravan with severe wounds to his back and hip and Krulac with a wound to his ankle.

Taking cover behind a parked white Dodge Caravan, Officer Guy sustained a severe injury also. A round hit him in the thigh, lifting him off his feet and propelling his leg up and in front of his face. It was a horrific wound and, had he not used his gun belt as a makeshift tourniquet, he would have bled to death in minutes. Trapped behind the white van, with bullets skipping all around, Guy and Detective Angeles, who had come to his aid although herself injured, would have to wait to be rescued.

The gunfire momentarily ceased when Phillips went back into the bank. After just a few seconds, he re-emerged, now with Matasareanu in the lead dragging the money bag. Six feet outside the door, their already-botched plan took another turn for the worse. The dye packs tucked in with the bundles of money exploded, staining everything inside a deep shade of red.

After briefly targeting those across the street, both made their way up the bank's walkway, abandoning the money as they headed toward the north parking lot. It seemed that their plan had changed from getting away with some loot to just getting away.

It was good timing. Guy was getting weaker and weaker, his requests for help fading. With less attention being given to targeting the civilians and officers across the street, two officers, Todd Schmitz and Anthony Cabunoc, formulated a plan to rescue Guy and Angeles.

Commandeering a police car, Schmitz and Cabunoc threaded their way through the parking lot to the waiting officers. Within feet of them, Cabunoc dove out and pulled the seriously wounded Guy into the back of the vehicle. Angeles scrambled into the passenger seat, and Schmitz accelerated the car in reverse. With Guy's wounded leg still dangling from the rear door and the sound of bullets zipping overhead, Schmitz maneuvered the car backward to a nearby parking lot where paramedics awaited.

Phillips and Matasareanu had reached the north parking lot after targeting Officers Conrado Torrez and Ed Brentlinger who had positioned their cars just north on Archwood Street. Both cruisers now sat abandoned, numerous punctures in their glass and sheet-metal skins. The officers had made it to better cover east of the lot, but not before each receiving injuries, Torrez a graze wound to the neck and Brentlinger shrapnel cuts to his face.

Over the radio, I heard that the robbers were now in the north parking lot and, incredibly, were not appearing to try to escape. With Matasareanu sitting in their getaway vehicle, Phillips was walking around targeting anything that moved.

Exiting the yard, I again turned north. Two dogs, eyes wild with fear, bolted past me in the opposite direction. I heard birds overhead and noticed that even they were fleeing the area. Everything felt as though it was on fast forward.

I joined some officers and detectives gathered in the street two houses up. It appeared that the backyard of this house would afford a good view of the bank's north parking lot. We made our way down the driveway, a wood and stucco garage ahead of us. Pausing momentarily next to the large garage door, three of us then continued around its peeling white paint corner toward the last bastion of cover between ourselves and the north parking lot, a cinder block wall. In a semi crouched position, with our guns at low ready in front of us, we rushed toward the wall.

My mind flashed, "These guys are shooting people with automatic weapons. What am I doing?" These thoughts had no effect on my actions though. I was on autopilot. I was doing what I was supposed to do. Reaching the wall, there were no emotions, no fear—just "Do it! Stop these guys!"

Slowly, I raised my head above the level of the wall, gun outstretched in front of me, hoping to see an unsuspecting target. What I encountered was far from it. There, just thirty feet away, was Phillips pointing the muzzle of his rifle toward us. Catching a glimpse of the tops of our heads, he had taken notice of our approach and waited until we were closer—close enough to take us all out.

Instinctively, I began to duck back down, but not before Phillips pulled the trigger on his rifle. There was no rat-a-tat-tat, no poetic gunfire sounds, but what felt like an enormous thunderclap, what it must be like to get struck by lightning. Ten rounds from his rifle zipped through the wall like it was butter; my face started to sting. I spun around and began a retreat back to the other side of the garage. Out the corner of my eye, I saw that my two comrades were alright, or so I thought, and doing the same.

As I made it around the corner of the garage, everything started to slow down, including the sounds around me. It was as though I was underwater. I stood leaning against the garage door. My face was still stinging. As I rubbed it with my hand, several pieces of cinder block that had been lodged in my skin fell to the ground. A peculiar *fft, fft, fft* traveled through the tree leaves above me, perhaps rounds from officers across the street missing their target?

A detective sat on the ground just to my right, blood streaming down his face from a superficial wound to his scalp. Looking down, I noticed several more pieces of the wall embedded in my uniform shirt. With everything still in slow motion, I thought to myself, "Am I in shock and in worse shape than I think?" I asked the officer nearest to me, "Am I okay?" His response was a quick "Yeah," followed by an intense, "They're coming through!"

For a second, I thought he was referring to the two robbers converging on our location. Snapping out of my slow-motion stupor, I looked to my right and realized that he meant the rounds fired by Phillips and Matasareanu were hitting the opposite side of the garage, going through everything inside and exiting through our side.

I had to move.

With news helicopters recording their every move, the robbers roamed the area along the north wall of the bank, Phillips firing at anything that stirred and anywhere he thought someone may be hiding. The question would be asked later, "Why didn't they just leave?" They had our backs to the wall. Why didn't they just get in their car and drive away?

My answer has always been rather simple yet surprising. I believe that Phillips was having fun. Loathing the police, he was having a field day cranking off hundreds of rounds at his favorite targets. Why leave the range so soon?

As for Matasareanu, a single bullet was about to change the course of the whole firefight for him. A solitary handgun round fired from an unknown officer slammed into Matasareanu's right buttock, dropping him to one knee. It seemed to take the fight out of him, and he retreated to the slightly safer confines of their white Chevy.

Phillips' murderous parade marched on. Walking along the line of cars, he continued his target practice. Whenever he raised his rifle, everyone ducked. After he unleashed a barrage and it was lowered, sporadic .38-caliber and 9mm rounds plinked back. Even the rounds that hit their target had no effect, though. The armor plate under his jacket and 43 pounds of Kevlar wrapped around everything but his head were deflecting everything. It was like trying to stop a stampeding rhino with a rubber-band gun.

Some have wondered why police didn't just shoot Phillips in the head. That's a topic I've have had to explain many times over the years. When both Phillips and Matasareanu were still in the parking lot, the nearest officers who had any decent view of them were at least thirty yards away. Achieving a head shot at that distance would be like getting one in the ten ring at the firing range. That would be hard enough. Throw in the facts that Phillips was a moving target, and you knew that right after taking your shots a torrent of rounds from a machine gun would be coming right back at you, and it's not as easy as it sounds.

While he was still in the parking lot, Phillips would also receive a wound that, though not taking the fight out of him, would hinder his mobility somewhat.

Standing at one point nonchalantly by the driver's door of the Chevy, he reached partway into the car for a new drum magazine being handed to him by Matasareanu. A police round slammed into his left hand in the soft spot between his thumb and forefinger. Tearing through the leather glove, the bullet traveled through the skin and muscle, breaking the thumb bone before exiting on the palm side. From then on, he would have to use the backside of his forearm instead of that hand to support his rifle. That was lucky for us, as it took away some of his ability to aim his rifle properly.

Phillips had a trunk full of weapons and ammunition from which to choose. He had been using the Norinco rifle for many minutes. With hundreds of bullets fired, it was getting overheated. He switched out the magazine one last time, slammed in a replacement 100-round drum and tossed the rifle in the Chevy's trunk. He then removed the HK 91, the civilian cousin to the HK G3, a battle rifle used by armed forces around the world. Illegally modified to fire in fully automatic mode like the HK G3, it was now used to spew out hundreds more rounds.

Phillips even took time out from his focused assault on us to target the news helicopters above. When his rounds streamed upward, the copters scattered, only to return quickly like mosquitoes on a warm summer night. At least one near-miss was reported as the choppers jockeyed for footage that would eventually be relayed around the world.

Two freelance photographers, Gene Blevins and Mike Meadows, had also made it to scene, capturing photographs that would later awe those who viewed them. A Telemundo News crew, Jorge Viera and Juan Guerra, moved a little too close to the action and almost became casualties themselves. They had made their way through the parking lot across the street from the bank, and their own video caught the sound of rounds ricocheting off a pole just a few feet from where they were taping.

Burbank Airport, three miles to the northeast of the shootout, rerouted its air traffic. Ten area schools were placed into lockdown. The Hollywood Freeway, just a mile away, was closed to traffic. Ten city blocks were eventually cordoned off as police officers from all over the city as well as other jurisdictions converged on the area. For the time being, though, and until SWAT arrived in the final few minutes, it was just us—a core of approximately twenty-five to thirty officers fighting to contain and stop the duo.

With our firepower not having much effect, the idea came to go to a nearby gun store, B&B Guns, for help. The rifles and ammunition that were "loaned" to some officers might have made a difference had they gotten to the scene in time. It was not to be, though. By the time the newly armed officers arrived, the gunfight in the parking lot had moved.

UNIFORM DECISIONS

As Matasareanu sat in the car, Phillips continued his merciless onslaught, but things were about to change.

CHAPTER TEN

ONE IN CUSTODY

As I hurried up the driveway and out of the yard, the calls for help from the officers who had been hit continued to stream from my radio. Forefront in my mind was "GO! GO! GO! I have to do something!" I was on fast-forward now with no clue about the effect the next three minutes would have on my life, what a major milestone it would be.

At the end of the driveway on Agnes Avenue, an unmarked police car with two North Hollywood detectives pulled up and stopped. Looking as though they were intent on joining us in the driveway, they seemed to change their minds when they saw several of us leaving the location so quickly. Reaching their car, I yanked the left backseat door open and jumped in, another officer doing the same on the other side. Without a word being said, it seemed we were all on the same page: Go north to try to get closer to the parking lot and head these guys off. The car leapt forward.

Still in the north parking lot, Emil Matasareanu had to be pleading with Larry Phillips to get in the car, "Let's go! Let's go!"

Phillips advanced toward their getaway car. With the HK 91 foregrip balanced along his left forearm, he fired round after round northwest along Laurel Canyon. Several news stations would later report that, during this time, he also fired into the car that Matasareanu was sitting in. Later examination of the vehicle and video would reveal that not to be the case. Confusion, especially for those watching the footage from a sky-high position, was rife. You can imagine what it was like on the ground.

Dean Haynes, still sheltered behind the tree only 200 feet away from the bank, continued to fire back, distracting Phillips' attention from targeting the civilians pinned down in front of him and the seriously wounded Martin Whitfield.

Richard Zielinski, another officer across Laurel Canyon and also north of the bank, took up the same tactic. Between the two, Phillips' attention was bounced from one side of Laurel Canyon to the other, effectively keeping the wounded safe from further onslaught.

During this time, two rounds from one or more officers struck Phillips' rifle, one of them smashing through the HK 91's magazine, rendering it useless. The second hit the front of the magazine well, bending the sheet metal inward and making the weapon incapable of accepting a new one.

That didn't stop Phillips, though. He threw the damaged rifle into the trunk and retrieved another. In a decision that would ultimately help doom him, instead of picking up his original Norinco rifle that he had used in the bank, Phillips selected the third and final rifle he would use that day: a different Norinco Type 56, a Chinese copy of the Russian AK-47.

Reacting to several bullets that struck him as he backed away from the trunk, Phillips ducked behind the bullet-riddled parked cars nearby. Rounds fired by officers ricocheted off the cars and wall surrounding him. With Matasareanu remaining in the Chevy, Phillips resumed his attack. Numerous rounds from his rifle streamed north toward officers and, at times, into the sky at the orbiting helicopters.

Possibly hearing over their police scanner one of the SWAT officers broadcast his intention to commandeer an armored truck that happened upon the area, Matasareanu again attempted to get Phillips into their car by flinging the passenger door open, but Phillips slammed it shut with his hip. Their window of possible escape was quickly closing. To further convince Phillips that it was time to leave, Matasareanu pressed on the gas and got the Chevy moving.

It was enough to get Phillips to take up a position next to it, and with him walking like an infantryman next to a tank, they proceeded north in the parking lot. They had begun their getaway.

Phillips' new armament had not been well chosen, however. This Norinco Type 56, converted to fire fully automatic, hadn't gotten the care and attention to detail that had been lavished on the other rifles. The extractor, the small piece of metal that aids in the removal of a fired cartridge, was badly worn. Failure to identify and replace this damaged $10 part helped seal Larry Phillips' fate.

Looking back, it becomes another one of those "what-ifs." What if his weapon had been fully functional? What if it had lasted just a little bit longer? What if...?

With Matasareanu slowly driving the Chevy, Phillips literally strolled along next to the passenger side. There seemed to be no urgency, no concern about not being able to walk away after all that had transpired. Turning northbound in the lot, they headed for the north exit. Pausing momentarily as their car stopped, Phillips threw the spare drum magazine he was carrying onto the roof. He then proceeded to rest his rifle on top of the car, just inches above Matasareanu's head, and open fire.

Once again, multiple rounds streaked through the air in the direction of the wounded civilians still cowering behind Dean's bullet-riddled cruiser. After several bursts, which must have sounded like a jackhammer to Matasareanu in the car, the worn-out part inside Phillips' rifle fouled for the first time, jamming it.

Their plan, which had slid off the rails from the first minute, was now on the precipice of total failure. The glitches were adding up, and though not giving us a tactical advantage, they were at least keeping us in the fight.

With his rifle jammed, Phillips peeled away from the car and moved twenty feet toward the parking lot's east boundary wall. Taking a knee by the side of a parked car, he frantically wrestled with the stoppage that his rifle had suffered. Matasareanu, seemingly leaving his partner behind, time and again took his foot off the brake and inched the car forward.

Several seconds elapsed, and after clearing his rifle and swapping the drum magazine, Phillips was ready to go again. Striding purposefully while spraying gunfire to the north and northwest, he caught up with and passed Matasareanu in the Chevy, who was on the verge of exiting the bank's parking lot to Archwood Street itself. The situation was deteriorating.

They were out!

Phillips, firing wildly from the hip, quickened his gait and moved along the dusty grass median along Archwood Street past Ed Brentlinger's shot up black-and-white. With several police rounds literally bouncing off his body armor, he moved toward a parked semi-trailer, casings from his rifle intermittently streaming out of its ejection port as he continued to fire. His bravado, his "come get me" attitude had changed, however. It seemed his actions and mind-set were now of a man running for his life, looking for a way out.

As Phillips proceeded along the median, it appeared that he was planning to catch up with Matasareanu again, but as he reached the tractor-trailer, another belch of smoke appeared as he fired another flurry. The biggest turning point in the day was about to occur.

Ducking behind the trailer, he raised the rifle. As he fired another burst of gunfire, his rifle jammed again.

As Matasareanu coaxed the wounded Chevy along the other side the trailer, fully expecting to meet up with his partner at the front end of it, Phillips reversed his steps and came back out at the rear of the trailer just in time to see the taillights of their getaway car disappear from view.

The Chevy continued, but with no sight of his accomplice, Matasareanu slowed the car near the front of the truck. He wouldn't remain there long, though. Completely unaware of his partner's problem, Matasareanu was about to encounter some of his own.

Officer Conrado Torrez, who had positioned himself just across from the parked tractor-trailer, observed Matasareanu in the waiting Chevy and began firing. One round passed through the open driver's window within inches of Matasareanu's face, clipping the rearview mirror. Startled, he stomped on the gas pedal and yanked down hard on the wheel, practically laying across the front seats in an attempt to avoid the incoming fire.

The Chevy lurched forward with renewed energy, bouncing hard off the curb twenty feet in the front of the truck cab. As it careened eastbound through the intersection of Archwood Street and Agnes Avenue, Phillips was left behind to deal with his own predicament.

Taking a knee at the rear of the trailer, Phillips yanked hard on the charging handle of his rifle in a vain attempt to clear the mess that was now jamming it. Without success, he moved underneath the trailer, searching for a safer haven to continue working on it.

The AK-47, and its subsidiary builds, are rifles renowned worldwide for their simple design and ability to operate in a variety of situations that would see other rifles fail. Their ability to work when dirty, corroded or covered in mud is well known. It's a rifle one could be confident of working even after dragging it from the bottom of a lake. Physical malfunctions are few and far between.

Phillips' current dilemma was unique, however. His rifle had experienced a very unusual stoppage. A round had twisted to the right as it came up off the magazine, jamming the bolt halfway open, and a spent casing that the worn extractor had failed to eject had become lodged under the trapped live round. Without field-stripping the rifle, it was, for the moment, useless.

Phillips worked frantically to clear his weapon, not knowing that within a minute he would be violently interrupted.

Only a hundred feet to the south of the intersection of Archwood and Agnes, the four of us crept slowly forward in the unmarked car. It was a journey that lasted maybe only ten seconds in total, but years later I can still recall it in detail.

We had no knowledge of the gunmen's exit onto Archwood Street. The radio traffic was cluttered and frantic. So much had happened in the previous forty minutes that it was hard to pin down exactly who was where and what was occurring. In the musty interior of the car, I could almost taste the rising adrenaline, and within its confines seeds of claustrophobia began to sprout. With all the bullets flying around and feeling like the robbers could pop out anywhere, I did not like being in that car.

"Let's go! Let's go!"

As far as I knew, we were the last chance for containing these guys. If they got past us, they'd be out into the neighborhood carrying an arsenal of weapons and ammunition, not to mention an already-proven mind-set of shooting anyone who happened upon their way. We needed to get into this thing and end it.

Our car crept forward and there in front of us, in a hurried flash of white, the bandit Chevy slammed into the curb and bounded through the intersection, its windshield perforated by at least four bullet impacts, its tires flattened. For a split second, I also caught a glimpse of the driver, a large figure in black.

A bowling ball of adrenaline bounced hard in the pit of my stomach. Finally, one of them was passing right in front of me!

Detective Vince Bancroft, our driver, kept a cool head. He didn't stomp on the gas to approach hastily. We were up against automatic weapons. To rush forward could have put us in a position of being in Matasareanu's shooting gallery, not to mention targeted by any other suspects possibly following nearby.

Vince pulled our car past two vehicles parked just south of the intersection and to our right, a red car and a white van. He nosed the undercover car into the southeast corner of Archwood and Agnes, just enough to see eastbound down Archwood Street, and then stopped. There, just a half block away, the flare of Matasareanu's vehicle brake lights came into view and it stopped as well.

I didn't see it, however. With only the ingrained practice of looking both ways before driving into or through intersections as reasoning, I looked to my left first, and what I saw kept my eyes transfixed.

There was some movement under a tractor-trailer parked at the south curb, a crouched figure in black. My first thought was that it was an officer, but I quickly realized otherwise. This figure was bulked out in heavy body armor, wearing a ski mask and holding a rifle, not quite normal police attire. It was another suspect, and possibly the one who had been pummeling the officers on the other side of the bank for the last half hour. It was Larry Phillips.

As he manipulated the rifle he was holding, it flashed through my mind that he was reloading to continue his attack, if not on those toward Laurel Canyon then toward us when we caught his attention. This was my chance.

There are times in life when you look back at something that you have done and ask yourself, "Why? Why did I do that?" For some, it's as innocuous as a new hairstyle or tattoo and the answer is as simple as "It was the new rage" or "I wanted to make a statement" or even "I had a little too much to drink." For other things, life-risking, life-changing things, the answer can be elusive and even a haunting reminder of something you'd like to leave in the past.

My only thought at the time was that I had a chance to stop one of these monsters and I needed to take it. Thinking about it afterward, I believe any other officer would have done the same thing if put in my position. In addition to it basically being "my job," fellow officers had been shot, pinned down. They needed help. The situation put self-preservation on the back burner.

In an instant, I yanked on the door handle. With nothing said to the others, I flung the door open and jumped out. Once again, I was on autopilot—no choices, no conscious decisions, just actions.

I was in a half crouch, my Beretta already in hand. A light breeze brushed my face as I quickly moved across the street. Nothing else seemed to exist, just the breeze and the monster in black under the truck. His back was to me as he continued to work on his rifle. I knew that I had only seconds before he would discover my presence.

As I stepped over the curb and onto the dusty corner of dirt and grass, I took two more paces, passing a fire hydrant on my left and stopping next to a short wrought-iron fence. Southbound on Agnes Avenue was out the corner of my eye. It was as close as I wanted to get to this guy. I was completely in the open and needed a way out if things went haywire.

I swung my Beretta up to a firing position and squeezed off the first round. With all that had been going on, I have to admit it wasn't lining up the sights in the ten ring, just point and shoot. The gun issued its reassuring crack, not once but six times, the recoil thumping back through my right hand and forearm. As I fired, I found myself taking a few steps backward and thinking about my escape route to the left.

I knew that some of my rounds had hit their target because Phillips spun toward me. His body armor had made them nothing more than a tap on the shoulder. I had jostled the beehive. Following the focus of his stare, the muzzle of his rifle crept upward.

I turned to my left in full flight mode, and right there in front of me was that fire hydrant. Only two feet high, it still stood as a solid monolith in the middle of my escape route. I anticipated the "blat" of the AK-47 from under the trailer and the impact of the rounds to take me off my feet. Would I feel it? Would I even hear it? The questions passed in the blink of an eye.

The gunfire never came, though. His rifle was still jammed, and with increasing attention coming down on him, he resumed feverishly working on it.

Without considering taking that extra fraction of a second to sidestep the hydrant now just one more step away, I completed a rather awkward hurdle over it and veered to my left across Agnes Avenue back toward the parked car and van to seek cover.

For a split second, I slowed to look over my shoulder to see where Phillips was, but having moved south on Agnes, I was now out of his sightline.

Within a few moments, I had sprinted across Agnes Avenue, making my way behind the parked red car and to a detective crouched at the front wheel of the white van. It seemed like good cover. I slowed to join him when

I noticed that the undercover car I had been in was just ahead of me, still on the corner and right in Phillips' line of fire. I didn't know it then but during my exchange with Phillips, the two detectives exited their vehicle, fired on Matasareanu's car, causing him to continue eastbound down Archwood Street, and had just reentered their vehicle to follow him.

All I knew was that Matasareanu was to their right and now Phillips was to their left. I had to warn them.

Running back into the open and toward their car, I had just reached it and was yelling to them there was another suspect to their left when Vince pressed on the gas to follow Matasareanu. Their car disappeared around the corner to my right, leaving me by myself once again. It felt like I was standing in the middle of an open field.

Out of the corner of my eye, I caught Phillips still moving around under the tractor-trailer, preoccupied with his jammed weapon. My Beretta came up to position and I began to fire, that familiar recoil buffeting my right hand. The rounds still seemed to have no effect, though, and he began to move toward the curb, out from under his temporary shelter.

I continued to fire as I made my way back to the cover of the van on my left. By mere chance, and unnoticed by me, I stopped firing just as the slide locked back on my now-empty gun.

Phillips knew the game was over. Shot in the left hand, right shoulder, buttock, scrotum and the left thigh, he was pretty badly, although not fatally, wounded. His mentality was later uncovered in an interview with his father, who claimed that his son had apparently said he "would rather die than go back to jail." Those were pretty strong words, but ones that Phillips was about to back up.

Larry Phillips exited the curb side of the trailer, turning east toward Agnes Avenue. His Norinco rifle lay abandoned in the road with an empty cartridge casing jammed in the ejection port pointing skyward, its own little monument to the devastation that its owner had wreaked on the neighborhood.

With his 9mm handgun now in hand, he turned toward us and began walking along the dusty median. Behind the white van I was using for cover, I didn't know he was heading in our direction.

Coming out from behind my position, I expected him to still be near the trailer. I made it a whole three steps before I realized exactly how close he had moved. There he was about thirty feet away, looking right at me. He seemed almost resigned to his fate. It was a second in time that I have played back over and over during the years with the same thought: It was as though he was saying, "C'mon, let's get it over with. It's you or me." In an instant, he raised his handgun and pointed it at me.

Had I tried to outdraw him, it wouldn't have mattered if I was as quick as Wyatt Earp. I still hadn't realized my gun was empty. For Phillips, it would have been like shooting fish in a barrel. Luckily, I decided to go for cover instead. His sights had just come up on me when I dove back behind the van I had just left. Three shots rang out, zipping through the air behind me.

As other officers' handguns began firing, I took a position over the white van's hood and noticed that Phillips, still armed, had stopped his advance. I took aim and pulled the trigger. It was limp, catching me off guard. I instinctively glanced down at my weapon as "gun malfunction" flashed through my mind, but it instantly became apparent that, "No, it's empty." After a quick duck behind the fender of the car, the empty magazine was clinking on the curb as I popped a new one in place and clicked the slide forward. I was now ready to go.

During my reload, another officer's round had struck Phillips' right hand, causing him to drop his gun. It wasn't a serious wound, but it was the final straw. The fight had left him.

Changing my position a couple of steps to my left and now next to another officer peering over the top of the parked red car, I looked for Phillips once again. Near the corner I had just vacated fifteen seconds earlier, he had bent down and was partially obscured by the wrought-iron fence. "He's reloading!" I thought.

When he stood back up, he had his gun back in his possession. Again I took aim. A maelstrom of bullets from not only me but several other officers began to pour in on him. Hot spent bullet casings began hitting me in the side of the neck as they sprung from the officer's 9mm handgun just to my left.

As during the entire incident up to this point, none of the rounds striking Phillips seemed to have an effect. He continued to stand there, gun in hand.

With bullets whistling toward him from several angles and news helicopters recording every second, one round would finally end his rampage.

At 9:56 a.m., Phillips put the muzzle of his 9mm under his chin and fired his last round. Death was instantaneous.

As he fell, several other police rounds struck him that would have been fatal had he not decided to take his own life. With more rounds slamming into the wrought-iron fence and others skipping in the dirt on the way toward their target, Lieutenant Mike Ranshaw, who had the best view of Phillips at that point, yelled "Cease fire!"

For a second, it seemed eerily quiet, a big change from the prior forty minutes. Just when my mental defenses began to relax, I heard a piercing whistle; a single, uninterrupted tone was saturating the scene around us. With all the unimaginable things that had transpired up to this point and the sound coming from the direction of Phillips' body, the thought of an explosive device ripped through my mind, a last send-off primed by Phillips during his final seconds to take out the unlucky cops who would storm in to take him into custody. Everyone held their positions. The truth was much simpler and quickly came to light: Just twenty feet behind where Phillips lay, a tire on the tractor-trailer had been struck by a round and was quickly losing its air.

With the whistle fading in the background, four of us, guns still at the ready, approached Phillips. It felt odd to be so close to someone who had been party to so much mayhem just minutes prior, including trying to take my life.

After struggling with the layers of body armor that Phillips was wearing, two of us were eventually able to get him handcuffed. Though he was deceased, it was protocol.

As Ed Brentlinger removed Phillips' ski mask, I think we were all a little surprised at what we saw. It's a snapshot I'll always remember. Without really thinking about it, I anticipated the look of your average scruffy, disheveled street criminal dirtbag. That was not the case. This career criminal who had just tried to kill so many looked remarkably clean-cut. With his shortly trimmed hair and somewhat European look, you'd never guess passing him on the street what murderous intentions were contained inside.

Backing away, I glanced to the sky. As a few puffy white clouds moved slowly overhead, the kind that are so white they demand a continued look, I reached back to my faith and thanked God for watching over us.

The long day's journey into the night had just begun. It was now guard duty at our location until the investigators and coroner would complete their jobs.

About a quarter mile away east on Archwood Street, however, Matasareanu's fate had not played out yet.

He was still running, trying to drive a car that was on the verge of mechanical collapse. After veering into two motorists in an effort to stop them and commandeer their cars, he tried a third. As with the previous two attempts, it failed, each time the motorists quickly driving away. This time, however, he exited his car and fired his rifle in the direction of the fleeing motorist.

As Matasareanu turned back toward his failing ride, he could have easily seen the knot of officers around his partner in crime. He walked around the front of his car to re-enter the driver's door and appeared to beat his chest twice with his right fist. Was it a salute to his fallen comrade? We'll never know.

After checking our immediate surrounding area for the possibility of more suspects or other type of threat, I began taking in the scene as a whole—the scattered bullet casings, the holes in the fence, the blood on the ground. Interrupting our scene, a dual-purpose police car pulled up next to us. It contained three SWAT officers. As I stepped off the curb, one of them asked, "Any more suspects?"

I pointed to my right. "Yeah, in the white car that just went eastbound."

They sped off, the tail of their Caprice squatting down and tires spitting up pebbles from the road.

With still a short time before their arrival, Matasareanu continued his efforts to commandeer a new ride. A civilian in a truck was his next target. As the truck approached from the opposite direction, Matasareanu veered his car toward its front. The driver stopped, but only long enough to realize that the other driver was no careless motorist but someone wearing a ski mask and holding a rifle. As he put his truck in reverse, it hadn't backed a foot or two before Matasareanu fired through his own windshield, hitting the windshield of the truck three times. Peppered with glass, the motorist abandoned his truck and took off running eastbound, making it to the porch of a house.

Matasareanu now had a new escape vehicle, but fate dealt him a bum hand: The truck's owner had flicked off the truck's fuel pump before he ran. Matasareanu would soon discover that he was going nowhere.

After firing a single shot westbound along Archwood to deter the patrol officers and detectives who had been shadowing him and stealthily attempting to close in, he tossed the Norinco he had used in the bank into the truck's open window. Returning to the Chevy's open trunk, with its flapping lid, he bent inside and retrieved the Bushmaster XM-15, complete with an attached 100-round Beta-C drum magazine.

The SWAT officers were just a few seconds away. Matasareanu climbed into the truck and used those few seconds in a futile attempt to start it. With no fuel pumping, he could have tried for an hour. It could not start.

With the SWAT officers' car now screeching to a halt right in front of him, Matasareanu made the same mistake that his partner in crime did. Instead of giving up when the chance of escape became nil, he chose to continue the fight.

The 6'2", 300-pound, wounded gunman bailed out of the truck and, showing a fleet foot for a man of his stature, ended up crouched by the front of his own car.

The SWAT car was parked mere feet in front of the truck. It was a bold maneuver so close to a suspect armed with automatic weapons—or so it seemed. In actuality, as the SWAT officers raced up, they thought that the figure in the truck was a citizen, not one of the gun-wielding bank robbers. Not until the last second did they realize whom they had rolled up so close to.

Both sides now had a measure of cover and concealment, and all hell broke loose.

Matasareanu released a barrage of relentless gunfire, most of the rounds recklessly penetrating his own car's windshield and still-open trunk. Several returning SWAT officers' rounds hit him square in the chest. Matasareanu sank from view; the steel trauma plate he had slipped into the front of his vest two hours earlier had just saved his life.

It was a brief and momentary reprieve.

Rising again, he continued to fire multiple shots in a wild arc. Residents along the street, some watching on their televisions as the battle raged just outside their doors, cowered in their houses as bullets crashed through walls.

Shots continued to ring out as another officer made his way to an angle left of Matasareanu. Every time an inch of the gunman's black jacket showed itself, he shot at it. Matasareanu was hemmed in. There was no way he could have escaped, but surrender was not on his mind. Yet.

Behind their car, the SWAT officers switched to another tactic. Lying down in the street behind their vehicle, they began to fire at Matasareanu's unprotected legs, riddling them with .223 bullets. Matasareanu still would not give up. It appeared that he would continue to his last bullet when, 144 seconds after the first shots were fired at this location, he dropped his rifle and raised his hands in surrender. The SWAT officers cautiously moved in, rolled him over onto his stomach and cuffed him.

There were now two suspects in custody. No one was sure there weren't any more.

Matasareanu, identifying himself as "Pete," was being completely uncooperative. Spouting obscenities, he refused to say if any other accomplices were involved and told the officers standing near him to shoot him in the head. His failure to cooperate eventually contributed to his own demise.

Suffering from a total of twenty-nine wounds, he would bleed to death in the street before medical attention reached him. With the threat of additional gun-toting suspects in the area, the ambulance response was delayed. Had he told the officers that it was just him and Phillips, he might have at least gotten to see a trial.

CHAPTER ELEVEN

ASSESSING THE DAMAGE

Pacing alongside the truck on Archwood Street, my adrenaline was still pumping. We had one suspect in custody at our location and another down the street.

It had only been a few minutes after Phillips was handcuffed and we had cleared our immediate area of possible additional suspects when I noticed the front door of a residence across the street from us slowly crack open. As I watched, I could see through the still-closed screen door a man's head cautiously peer in our direction. He didn't say anything, but I knew what he was thinking, "Is it over?"

His presence quickly reminded me that what had transpired over the last forty-five minutes wasn't known to all. It had been the entire world to me, the others involved and even some of those who were watching it televised across the nation. To the vast majority of people, however, including many just a few blocks away, it was just another day.

Then it hit me: Was my wife at work carrying out her usual responsibilities with no idea of what was going on? Was it still just another day for Lynn, or had she heard the news and watched the live coverage? Was she desperately trying to find out if I was okay or one of the officers reported wounded during the melee?

I needed to call her. I briskly trotted across the street toward the man in his doorway. Halfway there, I could see him looking at me with eyes as big as saucers. With all that had been going on, I'm sure the sight of some cop rushing toward him put who-knows-what thoughts into his mind.

I yelled, "Excuse me!" There was no answer.

When I reached the door, I could tell that he was somewhat shocked by my presence. "Could I use your phone for a minute?" The stunned look on his face melted away, and he snapped from his quiet, frozen stance.

"Sure!" He quickly opened the screen door and pointed me to a phone sitting on a table inside his living room a few feet away.

For a second, the quiet setting, with its relaxing furniture, mantle clock ticking and family pictures on the walls, struck me in its stark contrast to what I had just been involved with only a stone's throw from his front door.

Mindful that I needed to get back to work, I quickly dialed the number to my wife's office. I just needed to set her mind at ease that I was okay. When Lynn answered, I had only gotten out, "Hi, it's me" before she jumped in with her usual cheery voice saying, "Oh, hi honey. How's it going?"

Mixed feelings raced through me at that point. On one hand, there was relief that she had not seen or heard what had happened and wasn't worrying about me, but on the other hand, my mind was saying, "You've got to be kidding me! 'How's it going?' You don't know?"

I couldn't take the time to explain everything, so I told her only that something really big had happened. She would probably see it on the news, but I was okay.

As I made my way from the house back to the opposite corner of the street, Lynn made her way to her office break room. She walked in to find the television tuned to one of the news channels replaying a portion of the robbery shot earlier from their news helicopter. Though I had prepped her, the sight of me running around exchanging rounds with a guy with a machine gun caught her off guard. She also heard about the possibility of additional suspects still at large. Feelings of shock, anger and worry eventually gripped her, and as the day dragged on into night, my call of reassurance evaporated. There would be no respite until both of us finally made it home.

For me, the first few hours at Archwood and Agnes would fly by. I was glued to my police radio as reports of more possible suspects in the area, or even still in the bank, came in. Eventually, my instincts began telling me there were no others, that these two were it, and they were both in custody. To be sure, however, thorough searches still needed to be done. With assistance from several other law enforcement entities, ten city blocks had to be cleared.

Even with my mind racing over and over with what had just happened and how big this incident was, time then began to crawl and, unbeknownst to me at the time, give opportunities for the details of my surroundings to be forever etched in my mind: the bullet holes in the fences and cars, the jammed rifle discarded under the truck, Phillips' lifeless body, still handcuffed, laying in a pool of blood. These images, just to mention a few, would return unwelcome all too often in the future.

We did not have the scene to ourselves, though. Reporters were increasingly coming through to get their stories and photographs, and they needed to be watched and herded so as not to disrupt our crime scene and any evidence. Groups of the police department brass would also intermittently show up to take a look at what had transpired and what was happening now. Area residents and "lookiloos" were constantly trying to get close enough to catch a glimpse of something as well. All the while, the sound of news helicopters rained down on us. The scene began to take on a carnival-type atmosphere.

As nighttime approached, things began to let up and it was basically back to our original group at the corner, still waiting. For those who had fired their weapons, the Robbery Homicide detectives still had to show up and do "walkthroughs" with each of us to document our actions. The coroner's office also needed to respond and do its job.

ASSESSING THE DAMAGE

Finally, there was still the threat of additional suspects in the neighborhood. We knew we weren't leaving any time soon.

We took turns walking to a nearby Del Taco when we got hungry and were eventually relieved by other officers to wait inside a business two blocks to the south near the command post. At least now we could sit in chairs instead of on the curb. The room gradually filled with officers, those of us who had been on the front lines. It sounded like a crowded cafeteria, with guys relaying their stories to one another—what they had seen, what they had done, how they had survived.

Eventually, the detectives began their walkthroughs with us. One group at a time was taken back to our respective locations during the incident to show and tell exactly what we had seen and done. When they got to my group, nearly thirteen hours had elapsed since the shooting had stopped. The adrenaline was still pumping as though it had only been a few minutes though. This became more apparent to me when I returned to the corner.

It was very dark now, and very quiet. It was hard to see the bullet holes in the walls, fences and street signs. Police vehicles had been removed, some having been towed out of necessity. There were no more helicopters overhead and Phillips' body had been removed. It seemed peaceful now and not the place where you would guess a violent shootout had occurred just hours earlier. Standing there, somewhat daydreaming, I realized just how fast I was still going. My mind was racing, trying to recall, accept, categorize and file away all that had happened.

Catching me a bit off guard, a detective asked, "So what happened?" It was like the gate had just swung open at the Kentucky Derby. I rattled off only a few sentences before he interrupted and told me to slow down.

For the next fifteen minutes, I took him through everything I did—or so I thought. When I finished, we were standing at the curb on Archwood Street near where I had fired my last rounds. The detective scribbled some notes and then pointed over at the southwest corner, the corner where I had earlier jumped the fire hydrant to make it to cover. He asked, "What about over there?"

For a second, I didn't know what he meant, and in my mind I wanted to reply, "Well, what about over there?" Then I realized he was asking me to tell him about what I did at the corner. I hadn't told him I had even been there. With no recollection of being at the corner and a look of somewhat defensive confusion on my face, I blurted out, "I wasn't over there."

He looked at me with the same look that I must have given a hundred criminals in the past, one that said, "Are you trying to hide something?" He had seen the news coverage. Helicopters had recorded almost everything, including my actions, broadcasting them over and over all day long. He knew I had been at that corner, but not me. I couldn't recall.

Instead of challenging me, he calmly stated, "There are six bullet casings over there in the dirt that I think are yours." We walked over to the corner, and sure enough he pointed out six spent 9mm casings lying in the dirt. I thought to myself, "What? Was I here?"

I began to recall running to and from the corner but nothing about firing any rounds from there. I thought they had all been from across the street. I didn't want to sound crazy, so I told him that I had gotten a little mixed up but now remembered.

Unbeknownst to me, my mind could only absorb and handle so much so quickly. That part would have to wait. It would take until the next day, and some nudging by the news footage itself, to recall that part of my involvement accurately. Other more intimate details and thoughts would take weeks.

Soon after our group was done, and just before midnight, it was finally time to go home.

Fourteen hours after it all began, it was concluded that Larry Phillips and Emil Matasareanu were the only two involved and the search for additional suspects was called off.

An unmarked police van pulled up, and we loaded ourselves in. With most in our particular group now reaching their sixteenth work hour, the short ride back to the station was rather quiet. The silence in the air masked quite a different setting inside each of us, however. The reminders of automatic weapons being fired and desperate radio transmissions had already sprouted in our memories. I began to wonder how those who had been hit were doing.

Two civilians and eleven police officers suffered gunshot wounds. All would recover, but for two of the officers, the severity of their injuries would leave them unable to return to their careers.

It wasn't until the next day that the immensity of the devastation could be fully realized. There were hundreds of bullet holes in walls, windows, mailboxes, doors, utility poles. One concrete light pole was nearly sheared in half by the gunman's concentrated firepower.

Scores of vehicles showed scars of battle, among them Haynes and Whitfield's vehicles, both of which were complete write-offs. Haynes' vehicle was later counted to have been hit fifty-seven times. It is now stored in the Los Angeles Police Historical Society's museum, along with the gunmen's white Chevrolet Celebrity.

At final count, somewhere in the vicinity of 1,200 rounds were fired by Phillips and Matasareanu, with over 600 being fired by officers.

The broken windows, punctured vehicles, bullet casings, even the bloodstains would all soon be repaired, swept away and hosed down.

What would linger, however, were the effects from what all those who came in close contact that day would carry. For although the bullets had stopped flying, the North Hollywood Shootout was still not over.

My usual thirty-minute drive home took less than twenty, and I was greeted with a long hug from my wife. We both had stories to tell, but after a few minutes we realized that both of us were exhausted, mentally more than physically. Neither of us was scheduled to work the next day, so we'd have plenty of time to talk after a good night's sleep.

CHAPTER TWELVE

AFTERMATH

The next morning, Lynn told me that I hadn't slept well, waking her several times with what sounded like shouts of warning to others. I had no recollection of that and shrugged it off, not knowing this was just the tip of the iceberg of how the shootout would affect me. After about an hour of describing each of our "yesterdays" to one another and watching various pieces of news footage over and over again, I began to feel like I was missing out on what was going on at work.

The actual shootout was over, but I was still running at high rpm's and I knew the station was like a beehive of activity. I couldn't just sit at home and watch television all day. I needed to be a part of it, to talk about what had happened and get my engine to wind down. I had to go in.

While I was getting ready for work, Lynn was already out collecting newspapers from the local markets and convenience stores. The shootout was front-page news, and besides a sharp curiosity to find out more about the two gunmen, she had the quick foresight to think about how such memorabilia would be appreciated by our kids and future grandkids.

As I approached the station, it wasn't much of a surprise to see numerous news vans parked along the street with several reporters taping their coverage out front. After all, it had been like a modern-day OK Corral. What was a surprise, however, was the first greeting I got from one of my fellow officers.

There I was chomping at the bit to tell my buddies what had happened, what it felt like, and the first guy I saw asked, "What's wrong with you?" I looked at him in quizzical silence as he added, "How come you didn't use that pole for cover?" I quickly put two and two together and realized that he had seen some of the live news coverage and was commenting on a portion of my tactics while confronting Phillips.

Instead of getting a little support, I felt insulted, and my first reaction, knowing that he hadn't been present that day, was to reply, "I don't know, maybe if you'd been there you could have showed me." I held my tongue and laughed it off, though, telling him maybe I should have.

That exchange was the beginning of a realization that not all the attitudes of officers who weren't there that day would be positive. Some would be tainted with second-guessing born out of jealousy for not having been a part of a once-in-a-lifetime event.

The rest of the day went fast. Being there on a day off, I had the chance to hang around the station, and by talking to all the others I got what had happened a little better arranged in my head. When I arrived home that night, I was a little more relaxed. That was all I'd get, though. Things would start to catch up, to add up.

That week, our Behavioral Science Services people, the "shrinks," called us en masse to a get-together and very briefly went over what we could expect in regard to our individual reactions and feelings as time went on. When it came time for questions, there were none.

The mentality was "Cops don't talk to shrinks," especially in front of a room full of your cohorts. So that was it—no individual debriefing, just a few pointers, a business card and the opportunity to call them if we wanted to.

To this day, I consider that a big glitch in the department's handling of the event. I feel we should have had compulsory debriefing by a behavioral specialist. I, for one, had never heard of post-traumatic stress disorder. I know that many of us, though not actually diagnosed with PTSD, would not have had quite the rough roads we did if we had been properly debriefed and educated a little more in-depth about what to expect.

Back at the station, the press routinely contacted us, and numerous interview requests for television specials began coming in. In the beginning, most of us were happy to get involved. The department had told us it was permissible but also made it subtly known that we should watch what we say in the event there were any future lawsuits.

It seemed pretty ludicrous and offensive to me to think that anyone associated with either of these two criminals could make any money off them being portrayed as victims, but sure enough, a lawsuit was filed by one of the gunman's families regarding the handling of him after his arrest. Here we had officers wounded, almost killed, who were to suffer lifelong injuries, some requiring them to end their careers with the police department, and the criminal's family felt wronged. It was ridiculous.

The lawsuit was eventually dropped after the trial ended up with a hung jury—a hung jury! That meant there was at least one juror who sided with one of these monsters. It was a little shocking, not to mention maddening. An interesting twist was that the attorney who had handled the case for the plaintiffs eventually went to jail himself not long after for improprieties unrelated to the Bank of America incident.

In the months after the shootout, I found that any loud bangs or shouts took me for a jolt and movies with any kind of lengthy confrontation involving firearms would get me rattled to the point that I had to stop watching. I also became very critical of any reports regarding the incident. If it wasn't completely accurate or something was left out, I'd get mad.

On the flip side, one night I saw a short report about Larry Phillips' past that flashed a picture of him as a child on the screen. It really shook me up. My vision of him had always been one of a ruthless killer, but seeing him as a kid in those early, innocent years threw me for a loop. I found myself feeling bad—this for someone who had done so much harm to so many, including trying to kill me. How could this be?

The thing that affected me most, though, was that it seemed like I never stopped thinking about the whole thing. It was no different while I slept. Almost every night, I would either have dreams placing me back somewhere in the incident or wake up after just a couple hours of sleep and go over and over what could have happened, what should have happened, usually until the sun came up. It was getting a little ridiculous and having an increasingly negative effect on me.

Eventually, I took the Behavioral Science people up on their offer; I made an appointment. I planned to tell them what I had experienced and felt during the shootout and what I was experiencing now to see what they thought. Was this normal? That's all I needed to know. If it was, I could take care of things. But if it wasn't?

When I went to their offices, I found myself having to wait in a rather small and plain reception area. It was only a few minutes but enough time for me to start thinking about where I was. If anybody who knew me walked by, they would definitely see me in the shrink's office. The last thing I wanted was for someone to see me there and say, "Oh, hi John. You crazy too?"

Fortunately, that scenario did not arise and I was eventually invited inside by a woman holding a clipboard who seemed young enough to be my daughter. I wanted to get out of the waiting area in such a hurry that her greeting and title went in one ear and out the other, but I assumed that she was some sort of psychologist. We sat down in a small room, the door very conspicuously left ajar. I thought to myself, "I guess you guys need some quick backup at times, too."

I can't remember what was said first, but I found myself immersed in what I experienced on the day of the shootout, telling her with my inherited Italian animation and a quick, seemingly desperate voice every sight, action and feeling. When I finished, I became aware of my quiet surroundings and realized that I was sitting tensely on the edge of my seat.

I was looking at her for some sort of response, and after a couple seconds of silence, she said, "Okay. First off, I'm going to give you some breathing exercises that you can do." I thought to myself, "What? Breathing exercises? I don't want any breathing exercises. Didn't you hear anything I just said?" I expected some sort of acknowledgement, like "Wow, that must have been something," and maybe a little understanding of how talking about it could get me pumped up.

Instead, I felt like nothing I had just told her actually sunk in and that she didn't understand or maybe didn't even care. I skimmed over the rest of what I had planned to tell, not taking much note of what she said, and left with the feeling "That was a waste." So it was back to my dreams and the negative, critical thinking when it came to anything to do with the shootout.

My lousy attitude began to change in August of 1998. Within a two-month period, a flurry of ceremonies and events came up for those of us more intimately involved in the shootout, beginning with seventeen people receiving the following letter:

The Los Angeles Police Department is pleased to inform you that you have been chosen to receive the Department's highest award for bravery, the Medal of Valor.

Strict and demanding criteria govern this award. Candidates must have distinguished themselves by conspicuous bravery or heroism above and beyond the normal demands of police service through performed acts displaying extreme courage while consciously facing imminent peril.

The action you took and the risk involved reflects your high caliber as an officer. Your courage serves as an example to your fellow officers and to the community.

The Medal of Valor will be awarded to you on September 9, 1998, at the Medal of Valor Award Ceremony. Public Affairs Section coordinates this ceremony and will be contacting you in the near future to arrange for you and your family's attendance at the ceremony.

Signed by Bernard C. Parks, Chief of Police

Shortly after being informed of this honor, we began receiving congratulatory letters from the mayor, assembly members of the California Legislature, the United States Senate, the United States Congress and Vice President Al Gore, as well as local businesses.

On September 1, 1998, we attended The Los Angeles Police Historical Society's 5th Annual Jack Webb Awards. Held in the International Ballroom of the Beverly Hilton Hotel in Beverly Hills, it was an evening honoring "reel" cops and "real" cops, with celebrities such as Jack Nicholson, Angie Dickinson, Robert Stack, Charlton Heston, Ricardo Montalban and Steven Seagal in attendance.

The Medal of Valor events not only included the LAPD ceremony and Medal of Valor night at Dodger Stadium but also another one that caught me totally off guard: a surprise catered event that my wife threw at our home that included over forty relatives, close friends and coworkers.

It was a very busy time, all topped off when ten of us were selected to receive a TOP COPS Award by the National Association of Police Organizations. NAPO, founded in 1978, holds yearly ceremonies paying tribute to selected officers from around the country. From hundreds of nominations, one TOP COPS "case" from each of ten states is selected. Our families were flown to Washington, D.C., for a succession of carefully planned events and ceremonies that would end with a meeting with President Bill Clinton.

Arriving on a Wednesday afternoon, we were immediately met by a video crew that would shadow us for most of our visit, documenting our activities. We were taken by charter bus to the Omni Shoreham Hotel, a rather distinguished place often chosen by dignitaries, and basically given the rest of the night off.

Thursday morning, under the constant eye of video cameras, our group had breakfast together and then boarded a charter bus that took us to various sites and locations around Washington, D.C. The one that stood out most for me was the National Law Enforcement Officers

Memorial. Its inscription reads, *"It is not how these officers died that made them heroes. It is how they lived."* With over 14,000 names inscribed, it was quite humbling.

The day went fast, and early that night we attended a private reception held at our hotel for us to get to know some of the other officers and their families. The NYPD officers who had thwarted the then-recent attempted subway bombing were the most memorable for me. What a humorous and great bunch of coppers they were to hang around with! Another reception followed in a ballroom full of dignitaries, politicians and other invited guests. Ending the evening in another ballroom, we had dinner. Finally, it was time for the NAPO ceremonies, during which the award recipients were brought up on stage. As I listened to some of the stories of officers from around the country, it was once again quite humbling—this time to be included in such a group.

On Friday morning, we boarded our bus again and headed for the White House. Upon arrival, award recipients were taken to the Oval Office while our families were seated in the Rose Garden to enjoy the Marine Band. Walking through the White House was awe-inspiring in itself, but I will never forget standing in the Oval Office and soaking up the history that those walls had seen and heard. We shook hands with President Clinton, each having a minute or two to chat, and then met up with our families in the Rose Garden. President Clinton and U.S. Attorney General Janet Reno addressed everyone before making time for as many pictures as our group wanted.

Leaving the White House, we went to Phillips at the Marina Restaurant on the Potomac River for lunch, our last stop before heading home. It was a whirlwind of a few days and something I have continuously reminded myself that I was truly fortunate to have been a part of.

After getting back home, the critical attitude that I usually got with any reminder of the shootout was gone. I realized and focused more on how blessed I was in all that I had experienced and survived, not just the Bank of America incident but my whole career. How could I complain?

The LAPD also made some positive changes as a result of the shootout. Ballistic panels were put in police cars, ammunition was changed and every police division during any given watch now had at least one police unit equipped with a UPR, or Urban Police Rifle, a civilian version of the military's M16. Had there been one at 6600 Laurel Canyon Boulevard on February 28, 1997, the gunfight probably would have been over in the first few minutes. Also, Behavioral Science Services is now required to perform an evaluation of officers involved in a situation involving gunfire, including those present but not firing rounds.

My particular job was the same as it used to be. Still a Senior Lead Officer, I continued to address crime in my assigned area as well as to use the extra time gained by not getting assigned radio calls to work on the quality-of-life issues that residents brought my way. I had no problem in dealing with that. I knew how solving what would seem a little issue to an outsider was appreciated as eradicating a huge concern to those who lived there. It did strike me as interesting though, how sometimes people at the Business and Neighborhood Watch meetings that I addressed were more concerned and worked up about some trash that had been illegally dumped or some graffiti that had popped up in the neighborhood than with my reporting of an increase in car thefts or burglaries in the area.

In the position I was in, as rewarding as it was, time still began to take its toll. The dreams about the shootout continued. They weren't almost every night like they had been, but no more than a couple of nights could go by without me dreaming or waking up and thinking about what happened that day.

After a few years, the shine of the job was beginning to wear off again. Just like I had the last time as a training officer, I thought of promoting or transferring. This time was a little different, though. I wasn't being pushed by the unpredictable and routinely changing work schedule, the endless monotony of handling radio calls or loss of precious time with two little kids at home. My work schedule as a Senior Lead Officer was hard to beat. There were hardly any radio calls, and both my sons were now in their late teens and broadening their own horizons.

It didn't seem like that bad of a setup at the time. I coped with the dreams, and though I was a homebody with a beer in hand most of the time, as a family we still enjoyed more than the average share of outings and adventures. Did I really want to upset the apple cart at work? I decided against it, to just gut it out instead. In the quiet background, however, and not really being able to pinpoint why, my "gas tank" was getting full.

About this time, it also seemed that a pattern was evolving with officers I had worked with in the past taking their own lives, guys who had also been at the shootout. Three whom I had worked the confines of a patrol car with, whom I had joked with in the locker room and hallways during different periods of time, had decided that life was just too tough. These were guys I would never have dreamed of taking such action, guys who usually had smiles on their faces. I couldn't understand it, and though I had heard others, including the Chief, say that the shootout had nothing to do with it, I had my doubts. With my own baggage from the shootout as a backdrop, I easily saw how it could have played some part in the big picture. For someone to resort to suicide, it would require a lot of pressure and stress, two things the shootout was generous in providing.

Continuing my old routine, I would get through the day at work, go home, crack open the beers, go to sleep and start over the next day. That's the way it had been, and that's the way I thought it would continue. I knew it wasn't a good setup. A little voice in the back of my head frequently reminded me of that, but a little out of ignorance and a lot more in denial, I let a bad set of circumstances and this routine gradually take its toll.

I remained at the North Hollywood Division and on June 28, 2002, reached my twentieth year with the LAPD. Twenty years was a long time and so much had happened, but after the fact it seemed like it went by in the snap of a finger.

I kept that in mind. I still had time to do, and even though I preferred it out in the streets, I was now in my mid-forties. Suiting up and working in a black-and-white every day was becoming more of a challenge, not just mentally but physically too. Transferring to a position off the streets tickled my thoughts again. This time it wasn't for just a few seconds, as it had been years before, but something I had to consider seriously. A detective spot somewhere or a training assignment at the Police Academy were possibilities.

I never did get to make a decision.

CHAPTER THIRTEEN

OUT OF MY HANDS

It was August 25, 2002.

I usually didn't work Saturdays, but this one needed to be covered. I attended an event in a neighborhood in my area and then gave a personal safety presentation. It was a long day. I got home at around 10:30 p.m., exhausted, and was asleep by 11:00.

At 1:30 a.m., I awoke. This wasn't something unusual. Ever since February 28, 1997, if I didn't have the dreams, I'd wake up sometime during the night and rehash part of the shootout or an incident related to it. So I rolled over on my back and tucked my hands behind my head in preparation of what I thought would be a couple hours of sleepless monotony.

Before even a minute had passed, I felt a strange sensation around the inner left side of my nose and cheek area. It didn't go away, and instinctively I got up to go to the bathroom to blow my nose. After a few steps, I touched the left side of my face and was caught off guard with a feeling as though it had just been injected with a good dose of novocaine. My fingers felt as though I was touching a piece of Play-Doh. The expected connection wasn't there. As my fingers probed further, I began to realize that the entire left side of my body was going numb.

I had no idea what was going on at that point and no time to think about it before I started feeling dizzy to the point where I thought I'd throw up. I didn't know whether to stumble back to the bed or make it to the toilet. With my head now spinning and standing becoming a challenge, I took the shortest route and plunked myself down at the foot of my side of the bed. I was still extremely dizzy, and my concern about what was happening started to sink in.

I reached over and shook Lynn's foot, waking her up. I got right to the point: "Something is wrong, and I think I need to go to the hospital." With the bedroom light now on, Lynn could see that the right side of my face was not moving as I spoke.

That's when things kicked into high gear. I needed to get to the hospital, fast!

My two sons helped load me into the car, and Lynn and I were off to the emergency room. It was a short drive, and with the dizziness subsiding a little (or maybe I was getting used to it), I walked in with little help. The waiting area appeared half full with an array of people of different ages, some still in their pajamas. For a moment, I wondered why they were there—a cut on the finger, a twisted ankle, a sprained wrist? Nothing that came close to having half your face frozen and no feeling on the entire left side of your body, I thought.

I gave the receptionist my information and after a short wait was taken to a triage room, where a nurse took down my symptoms. With the place doing a brisk business, including a heart attack victim they were working on, I was put on a gurney in the hallway and, with Lynn standing next to me, told that it would be a little wait. As I lay there, I started to think about all the times I had responded to radio calls and hospitals where it was always the other person lying on a gurney. Now it was my turn. It gave me an odd feeling of helplessness.

After a few minutes, I felt a wave of the extreme dizziness start to come over me again. This time it was much worse. I got Lynn's attention, and all she could do was watch as my eyes started to roll and my body convulsed with dry heaves due to the sickening spinning in my head. Lynn ran down the hall to get someone to help me. With no doctor available, a nurse came back with her.

By the time they arrived at my side, the wave had subsided, but not without leaving a change in the landscape: Added to my symptoms were now the inability to swallow and no sight in the left side of each of my eyes. I was in real bad shape now.

When a doctor eventually checked me out, he quickly deduced that I had suffered a stroke. When he told me, at first it didn't really sink in. I had no response. I remember thinking, "Okay, what now?" The fact that I could remain in this condition for the rest of my life, or maybe even get worse, never entered my mind.

Behind the scenes, Lynn was getting the ball rolling. She wasn't going to let them just give me some aspirin and roll me down the hall into a room. She made some calls to the police department and, with help from fellow officers and acting Chief Martin Pomeroy, was able to set up helicopter transport to the UCLA Medical Center, even though UCLA had reported to be "full." My flight never got off the ground, however. I went by ambulance after the trauma nurse accompanying me advised that the hospital's insurance didn't cover their employees flying.

At the time, it made no difference to me. Everything seemed so surreal, and on top of everything, I was preoccupied with the constant accumulation of saliva in my mouth and my inability to swallow.

When we got to UCLA, I was rolled into a very busy admitting area where I was to wait for an open bed. It was now late Sunday night, almost twenty-four hours after shaking Lynn's foot and beginning this odyssey. We were both exhausted. At least I got to lie down, but after about an hour of waiting, it was apparent that Lynn had to get some sleep. I didn't want her to go, but I convinced her it was no big deal and that I'd be alright. Hating to do it but needing the sleep, she left for the night.

Now I felt alone, and it hit me like a ton of bricks. With strangers all around and in the condition I was in, I felt very vulnerable, a feeling I was in no way familiar with.

Eventually, I was taken to a room that would be my home for the next five days. During that time, I was subjected to numerous tests. The doctors knew I had a stroke and that the blockage had occurred in my brain stem, but they wanted to identify what caused it. My weight was never a problem. My blood pressure and cholesterol readings had tipped the scales a few times in the past but, considering my age, that was nothing major. Job stress and my beer drinking stood out. Overall, however, I was in pretty good shape. When all was said and done, they couldn't pinpoint anything. Physically, except for the stroke damage, I was healthy. All they could say was that it was likely a combination of the various factors and, in my doctor's own words, "a fluke."

From the first phone call that Lynn made to my work about the stroke, we were treated like family. The Employee Assistance Unit offered to transport Lynn between the hospital and home every day. Though our sons were older, child care and transportation between their schools and home was offered. They gave Lynn assistance with hospital, workers' compensation and payroll paperwork to ensure that the bills and payments would be sent to their proper places and not pile up in our mailbox. The department really took care of us.

While still in the hospital, I got just as many visitors as I could handle. Most were guys that I had worked with, but some were citizens I had helped in the past who caught wind of my situation. They wanted to return the favor.

It was one of those times when news spreads quickly, and within a couple of days both Lynn and the police station started to get numerous phone calls inquiring about my situation and offering support. The station could handle it, but Lynn was inundated. Before "blogs" had become mainstream, she began posting a daily journal on a website for those who were interested. Besides the benefit of keeping everyone updated without becoming overwhelmed, Lynn found that writing each evening was cathartic and helped her sort out what had gone on that day. It brought the hectic swirl of trying to handle everything down a notch.

Also helping was Lynn's mother, Delois. She dropped everything to come to our house and stay with Lynn until I was released from the hospital. Her gentle prodding ensured that my wife ate right, slept enough and kept a level head.

My own situation remained the same. The doctor mentioned a couple of medications that I would continue to take to prevent another stroke. Then they told me that, as far as getting back any of the physical abilities that were lost or damaged, only time would tell and that ninety percent of whatever healing I might experience would happen within the next six months. Further improvement, if any, would be over the rest of my lifetime. Those weren't very comforting words at the time. Besides the facial paralysis, left-side numbness and eyesight limitations, I couldn't swallow. How would I eat? The thought of living off fluids squeezed into my stomach through a tube permanently inserted through my nose and throat was rather depressing.

It would be another day and a half before I would be discharged, which gave me a lot of time to think. It was then that the big picture began to come into focus. What had happened wasn't a fluke but a wake-up call. Ever since high school, there had been a tapping on the shoulder, that little voice, a calling to give attention to that back burner where my Christian beliefs and faith had been relegated.

Now I realized that life wasn't just about making money, keeping a roof over my family's head and enjoying what I could. It wasn't all about what I wanted, but what God wanted. He was supposed to be in charge. I had dodged that fact and its acceptance for so long that it took a good smack upside the head and bringing me to my knees to finally listen and give up the helm. When I did, two areas in my life immediately came to mind. Not that they were new issues. Over the years, whenever I had gotten that tap on the shoulder, that nudge, both were there at the front of the line and were routinely sloughed off. Now was commitment time, though, and God had set up a little groundwork to help me out.

First, drinking almost every day would be a thing of the past. If I had ever said that to myself during the prior twenty years, my next thought would have been a resounding "No can do!" This time was different. Not being able to swallow—anything—made it pretty easy to initiate. Using alcohol as a crutch was over.

Secondly, regarding my faith and God's will in my life, the excuse "I don't have time" was out the window. Getting my health back would take a while. I would have all the time in the world now. As far as how I'd gotten to this point, I had chosen the hard route—one not necessarily required for everybody, but better the hard route than no route at all.

After six days at UCLA, I was released on a Friday to go home. To give Lynn a break, a buddy of mine from work picked me up in a black-and-white. Riding in the police car, unshaven, looking a little thin and pale and with a hospital tube coming out of my nose, I must have been quite a sight. Several people catching glimpses of me got looks on their faces that seemed to say, "What did the guy do to deserve that?"

My first day home was somewhat of a shock to Lynn and the kids. They had all visited and seen me in the hospital, but now I think the realization of my condition really set in. I needed to have daily shots of blood thinner injected into my abdomen. Eating meant hooking up a syringe to the tube I had coming out of my nose and squeezing formula into it. Not being able to swallow necessitated spitting out saliva whenever it accumulated. It was a depressing scene.

After just one day, the thought of being this way for the rest of my life began to gnaw at me. Just before bedtime and feeling really low, I reminded myself that God was the one in control now. Saying our own short prayers to ourselves before turning out the lights, Lynn and I were on the same page: However I ended up, it would be God's choice and for His glory. I have to admit that my prayer did have a preference, though. With only fluid intake for the past week, I felt like I was starving. I wanted to chew something, taste it, swallow it and feel it in my stomach. The bottom line, however, was "Not mine, but His will."

It was only a couple of minutes before I noticed something had changed. My throat felt different. It was nothing specific, but something gave me the urge to see what was up. I turned the light on, and from a bottle of water Lynn had on her night stand I let a trickle roll to the back of my tongue. Up until this point, anything like that triggered a little bit of a choking reflex, as the muscles in my throat were paralyzed. This time, however, the water was gingerly massaged back and down my esophagus. Another try and the same thing happened. I was swallowing! The timing of this could not be written off as coincidence or luck. It was an answer to prayer!

Lynn called the doctor the next morning to give him the news and ask if I could remove the feeding tube myself. Sounding a little incredulous at such a quick recovery, he still gave the okay. By that night, I was eating soup, and over the next few days Lynn made many of my favorite foods, each bite and taste relished as I never had before.

I remained off work for a year. Besides the ability to swallow, I got back near perfect eyesight as well as ninety percent of the use and feeling that parts of my body had lost. I was truly blessed.

Throughout the year, guys from the North Hollywood Station continued to visit me and help make sure I didn't get bored. One day, they brought me a kit to build a model of an eighteenth century British warship. It took several months to complete and stands on display in our home today, a reminder of the friendship and support I received.

When I returned to duty, the medications that I took prevented me from working the streets any longer, something that I did come to miss at times. I spent another seven years in the North Hollywood Division's

Community Relations Office before retiring in 2009 with twenty-seven years of service in the department.

It was quite a ride, replete with its fair share of extraordinary sights, experiences and life-and-death scenarios. Police work is a career that could easily and stealthily take center stage in one's life. You could ask almost every new officer I ever worked with and they would probably recall me telling them, warning them, "Don't make the job number one in your life." During my career, I did quite well at practicing what I preached except for one thing. Even though the department wasn't number one in my life, what was? The decision to not let my career be the main focus of my life was important, but even more important was my decision to finally listen to and act upon that little voice calling me, a voice that calls for everyone at some point in time and one I would suggest not ignoring.

CHAPTER FOURTEEN

A CHANGE OF SCENERY

It's a couple of years after leaving the department, and Lynn and I are celebrating our thirty-fifth wedding anniversary with a trip to Europe. Enjoying the sights and tastes of Italy, France and Spain, two weeks seem to have gone by in the blink of an eye. We're settled back into the seats of our Air France jet as it taxis down the runway for the eleven-hour flight home. I pause again, as we both have done several times these two weeks, to remind myself of and be thankful for how fortunate we are to be able to enjoy this trip together, our lives together.

As I lay my head back on the headrest, our takeoff is strikingly smooth. With a cool, air-conditioned breeze wafting over my head, I close my eyes, hoping to catch some sleep. The plane banks under me and catches the afternoon sun. Through the window, it blankets my face with warmth.

I'm close to falling asleep. The wing catches an air pocket, sending a slight shudder through the plane, and my head rolls on the headrest. My heart rate increases, and I find myself now standing, standing on a street corner. What is this? I look up to see a street sign: Archwood and Agnes!

I'm dreaming, and it's a dream I know all too well. I want to wake up, but I can't. More of my surroundings begin waving, misting into focus. How many times have I been through this?

Something is different, though.

The street is quiet and sedate. Gone is the tractor-trailer unit; there are no black-and-whites, helicopters, spent bullet casings littering the ground or frantic radio calls. It's just me, a cool breeze and the warmth of the sun on my face.

I look over toward Laurel Canyon Boulevard. Traffic hums past, unconcerned with my presence. Archwood Street is empty; there is no sound of gunfire or monsters in black to contend with. Birds are chirping in the trees, and everything is so peaceful. The barbed hook of the past has lost its hold, and the ghosts have faded to remain just faint remembrances now.

I turn a full 360° looking around. Any stranger walking these streets would have no idea what happened here on that day in 1997. Except for a few patched bullet holes in a cinder block wall and a couple more in a wrought iron fence, nothing remains as a testament to the carnage that once dominated this spot. Peace and quiet rule the roost now.

I turn my face upward to soak in the warmth of the sun. Again I feel a shudder, and my surroundings start to fade.

"John." I slowly open my eyes and see Lynn looking at me, a mixture of concern and curiosity etched on her face. "You okay?"

With the vestiges of a smile toying with the corners of my mouth, I whisper, "Yeah, everything is fine."

EPILOGUE

The crucible that is an officer's career is one beset by many and varied challenges, it takes a special breed of person to master that role. In 1929 Ernest Hemingway wrote, "The world breaks everyone, and afterward many are strong in the broken places." Twenty-seven years as a first responder is going to leave a mark on anyone, and John Caprarelli is no different. The John that lives quietly and humbly in his active retirement today still carries the scars of his service, yet he carries them well and with a dignity born of the realization of the price he paid for them; they seem to suit him somehow. As part of a close-knit family, John, his wife Lynn and their two sons all took some hefty bumps from John's life as an LAPD officer. They all made it through, and that is refreshing to see.

Since 2002, many opportunities have opened up for John and Lynn, opportunities for them to speak publicly about their individual sides of life behind the badge. They've been invited to speak at various venues regarding the Bank of America incident and how it affected their lives. Those presentations are a mixed blessing, for within them there is a chance to educate on the dangers of hidden job stresses, and how to get the often-needed help for them, yet in telling the story with the aid of a short documentary-style film, the sound of fully automatic gunfire tugs at the memories of a day that really was just too close for comfort.

Lynn began the LAPD Wives Association in 2005, a group for wives of LAPD officers that provides support through friendship, education and experience. This led to the formation in 2006 of the national Hidden Partners organization, which assists wives of first responders in starting and maintaining support groups. All too often the people behind those in uniform go unseen. Their efforts to maintain a healthy, stable home in the face of a stressful lifestyle can be monumental, however. With the national divorce rate for law enforcement officers running up to as high as seventy-five percent, education and support of these families can be nothing but a positive thing.

John has addressed various police support groups as well as church organizations and young adult groups. With his involvement in the shootout and its aftereffects always a big draw for audiences, his message continues to be a steady reminder of the importance of focusing on faith and family.

What good are our lessons if we do not use them for teaching? John and Lynn continue onward, their mentalities geared toward helping people in the same situations they once found themselves in, adding a friendly human touch to an honorable cause.

I met John and his family through an associated project at the start of 2011. For several years, I had been building a website that attempts to give a true and impartial telling of the story of the North Hollywood Shootout. The Caprarelli family felt that the timing was right for John's story to become public. After several weeks of discussion, we embarked on a process that was new to us all. Eleven months later and here we stand, ready to close the last page and hand the book over to you, our readers.

A phrase that sprang up in early conversations comes back to me now, a phrase John uses to describe an officer's career: riding the bullet. In closing, I can say only one thing about his amazing journey: "One bullet, well ridden!"

Lee Mindham

With Lynn and co-author Lee Mindham, October 2011

Resources

Uniform Decisions
www.uniformdecisions.com

Bears in the Beehive
www.northhollywoodshootout.com

Los Angeles Police Historical Society
www.laphs.org

National Association of Police Organizations
www.napo.org

Hidden Partners LEO Wives Associations
www.hiddenpartners.org